These Ruins are Inhabited

MURIEL BEADLE

These Ruins are Inhabited

ROBERT HALE · LONDON

© *Muriel Beadle 1961*
First published in Great Britain 1963
Reprinted 1963 (twice), 1964 (twice), 1965, 1966, 1967, 1970, 1975
and 1981
First paperback edition 1989
Reprinted 2003

ISBN 0 7090 3517 9

Robert Hale Limited
Clerkenwell House
Clerkenwell Green
London EC1R 0HT

The right of Muriel Beadle to be identified as
author of this work has been asserted by her
in accordance with the Copyright, Design and
Patents Act 1988

A catalogue record for this book is available from the British Library

2   4   6   8   10   9   7   5   3

Printed by
Gutenberg Press Limited, Malta

To GEORGE and REDMOND

For many reasons, not the least of
which is gratitude for their patience
while the book was being written

Acknowledgements

THE author expresses her thanks for permission to reprint 'Tourist's Round', from *Culex's Guide to Oxford* (The Abbey Press, Abingdon, Berks.); and to quote from the following: George Mikes's delightful guidebook, *How to Be an Alien* (André Deutsch, Ltd., London, 1946); 'Oxford Letter,' by Glen W. Bowersock, in *The American Oxonian*, July 1960; and *Other Schools and Ours*, Edmund J. King's excellent study in comparative education (Rinehart & Co., New York, 1958).

It should also be mentioned that some of the material in this book has appeared in different form in *The Saturday Evening Post*, in *The American Oxonian*, and in *John Bull*.

Chapter 1

NOW THAT THE TRAIN was slowing down and the rain was no longer slashing so fiercely at the windows, it was possible to see something of the countryside through which we were passing. The scene was drab, small farms and pastureland beginning to give way to clusters of brick buildings and back-yard cabbage patches. Ahead I could see some metal sheds and a storage tank. *It looks like the outskirts of Peoria*, I thought. *And it mustn't.* This was the place that Dryden had likened to Athens, and Hazlitt to Rome; this was Max Beerbohm's lotus-land, Logan Smith's 'taste of Paradise'. *Please don't let it look like Peoria.*

There was a little stir outside our compartment as disembarking passengers began to form a line in the corridor. My son, Redmond—a lanky near-fifteen, and by his own measure as good as grown up—unfolded from his seat, stretched and said, 'Well, I'd better be getting the suitcases down. This *is* Oxford, isn't it, Mom?'

'I guess so,' I replied, my eyes still searching the landscape ahead. 'It's silly of me, I suppose, but I was hoping . . .' And then I saw them. The towers of Oxford. Square, rounded, tapered, like fingers lifted to heaven. Blurry in the mist, but there; and we were going *toward* them. It was only a glimpse. They speedily vanished behind a chain of trackside buildings. But it was enough. 'Yes, Red,' I said—and now my voice was confident and cheerful—'this is Oxford. What are you going to carry, and what shall I take?'

As we dragged our luggage out into the corridor, I said, 'I wish Pop were here, don't you?' George was in London, touring a lab, and would drive out later in the day. I was sorry that we weren't sharing the moment of arrival.

Red shot me an indulgent glance; my menfolk know that I am sentimental about beginnings. 'It isn't Plymouth Rock, Mom.'

'I know, but even so . . .'

To an American academic family, coming to Oxford was like coming to Olympus—exciting but scary. We were there because my husband, geneticist and professor of biology at Caltech in Pasadena, had accepted a year's appointment as a visiting professor at the university. I had without regret quit my own job as a newspaper reporter in order to accompany him to England; and Red had beat his brains out for nine months in preparation for the school that awaited him here. Those spires up ahead symbolized the grace and beauty and intellectual richness of England's oldest university—some of which we hoped would rub off on us.

The Oxford station was a dark and smoky bedlam. We followed the crowd, sucked along as if by a giant syphon, toward a slotted gate. As we neared this bottleneck, staggering slightly under the weight of our luggage, a brawny young man with a knapsack on his shoulders tried to wriggle past us. He whacked his shin against the suitcase Red was carrying and spun us both into the path of a tall, lean man whose sandy moustache seemed to quiver as he checked his own forward motion.

Even as I apologized, I was cataloguing him: bowler, dark jacket, striped trousers, leather gloves, neatly furled umbrella carried canelike in his right hand. *Ah, an English gentleman!* He acknowledged my 'so sorry' with a faint inclination of the head and a dilation of the nostrils. Then he squared his shoulders against the pressure of the crowd behind us and moved off again, this time lifting out of harm's way the burden he had been carrying in his left hand: a brace of pheasants. *Probably bagged them at his shooting lodge,* I decided, pleased by this early encounter with the landed gentry. As I think about him now, the probability is that he was a college porter doing an errand for the chef.

I remain grateful to him, however, for the romantic touch he added to our arrival in Oxford. It was the only one. Where were the quaint old inns with cobbled courtyards and window boxes full of flowers? The grey-walled colleges with coats of arms above their fretwork gates? The dons strolling in the groves of Academe? This was a city of dirty, no-period buildings, of narrow streets choked with traffic, of store fronts like those in small towns in Nebraska. Nothing appeared as in the Come-to-Britain ads except the big red buses chugging along the same route our taxi took from the station to the suburb of Headington.

Nor did our new house (supplied by the college with which George would be affiliated) look quite as much like Anne Hathaway's as I had thought it might. It had been described in correspondence as a stone cottage, but no gate bowered by roses awaited my hand, no patch of lawn or border of fragrant pinks met my eye. In fact all that separated the house from the street was a lean strip of sidewalk, decorated at the moment by a couple of candy-bar wrappers. Nothing separated the house from its two neighbours; they shared common walls, ours rising higher because it had a second storey. Aside from the fact that it had recently been painted Bermuda pink, it was a no-nonsense stone box, devoid of frills.

The frills were inside. The living-room was, at first glance, so overwhelming that what the landlady looked like and what she was saying failed to register. The room was so *little*. So full of *things*. Samplers under glass. Della Robbia plaques. Venetian water colours in heavy gilt frames. Corner cupboards stuffed with porcelain. A wall of books. Lamps with lace shades and velvet bows. A ship's clock. Ceiling lights with crystal drops. Red brocade draperies, red damask chair seats, red and white pillows, red chintz slipcovers. Oriental rugs. Striped wallpaper. Pattern rampant everywhere.

But even as despair mounted, I recognized the effort that had been expended to make us welcome. Everything was spotless. The woodwork was freshly painted. The brasswork gleamed. Table tops were mirror-bright. A glorious bouquet of Michaelmas daisies stood in front of the fireplace. Shame overwhelmed me, and with a contrite heart I turned to our landlady. Maybe if I concentrated on *her* instead of the house . . .

She was a tall woman, bigger-boned than the English women I'd previously met, and so regal of manner that Lady Headington seemed a much better name than her own. She was saying, 'The clock should be wound once a week, you open the crystal with this key and wind with *this* one; and that's really all that needs looking after in this room. Except for the barometer. It must be kept upright'—she was talking now to Red—'at all times. Is that clear?'

'Yes, *ma'am*,' he said.

We followed her then into a tiny enclosure that served to link the house with a shedlike wing projecting to the rear. 'This is the solarium,' she said proudly, 'I'm leaving my plants for you to enjoy.' The room had a corrugated plastic roof and one glass wall, and on the others there were pots of geraniums, ivy, and other pendant vines; a jungle of them. A two-foot lemon seedling and some ferns occupied pots at our feet. My thumbs, never too green, paled further, but I murmured, 'How nice!'

She led us upstairs next—the risers were so high and the treads were so narrow our heels hung over when we climbed—to the two bedrooms and the bathroom. None of these was rectangular. The wall facing the bathroom door was so sharply angled the door barely cleared it. The bedrooms had bays and setbacks, filled-in fireplaces, and remnants of beams: evidence upon evidence that various owners had done a lot of tinkering.

'How old is this place?' I asked, noting a frayed sash cord in Red's bedroom.

Lady Headington shrugged. 'Oh, a hundred and fifty years, I dare say. Maybe two hundred. Your son will be careful with this chest, won't he? It's a Chippendale I'm rather fond of.'

The doorbell rang.

In a minute she called me down. There, with a bouquet of flowers in his arms, a worried look on his face, and a desire to know whether the house was satisfactory, stood Mr Bennett, the domestic bursar (that is, the business manager) of Balliol College, who had rented it for us. I had never been presented in person with a sheaf of flowers; in my experience this sort of thing is a prerogative of prima ballerinas. So I was too effusive as I thanked him, which made him even more nervous.

His jumpiness was understandable. Oxford had recently had in residence some rather difficult—and vocal—American wives, and for all the bursar knew I might be another. Signs pointed in that direction: among the spirited letters we had exchanged was one from me saying that I would not accept a house without central heating, and one from him saying that the best house he could find—this one—didn't *have* central heating. So here we were.

'Have you had a chance yet to check the silver?' he inquired. I hadn't, so we did it together. What a table I was going to set! The college had sent up a complete service for twelve: luncheon forks, luncheon knives, dinner forks, dinner knives, teaspoons, dessert spoons, serving spoons, coffee spoons, fish knives, fruit knives, cheese knives, carving knives, teapots, coffeepots, water pots, mustard pots, jam pots, cruets, sugar shakers, salt cellars, serving dishes, big pitchers, little pitchers, trays, toast racks, and—whee!—a bucket for icing champagne.

It was only after Mr Bennett had bowed himself out—allowing himself a frosty smile on departure—that I realized that the dining-room table would seat, at most, six people. And that the dining-room was so located that guests would have to pass through the kitchen to get to it. The possibility of our giving formal dinner parties suddenly grew very remote.

The kitchen and dining-room were housed in the wing that the 'solarium' linked to the house. Both rooms had casement windows along their entire length, and were light and open and inviting. Under the kitchen window was a six-foot table—the biggest unobstructed expanse of surface I'd seen in the house—and my eye lit on it with joy. But what my gaze lingered on was a large, buff-coloured, enamel range, its back guard and black flue pipe towering ominously over an iron cook-top. Surely this was the 'solid fuel cooker' about which Mr Bennett had written me. ' "Solid fuel cooker", indeed!' I had said to George. 'I'll bet it's a plain old coal stove.' And so it was, as one glance at the scuttles standing beside it confirmed, except that the cooking surface on the top was a metal plate with a hinged enamel cover.

Lady Headington called it 'the Rayburn', and proceeded to instruct me in its care and feeding. It was not only a cooker but also a source of our hot water, she said. She showed me where the water pipes left the firebox, arching up the wall and travelling behind the shelf over the sink, finally to disappear in the greenery of the solarium; they emptied, she said, into a tank in a closet off the living-room.

Flinging open the Rayburn's upper right-hand door—'Jolly little fire in there now, you see'—she armed herself with a pronged metal handle, hooked it into a rod, and shook down the fire, thus releasing a cascade of sparks and glowing coals into the ashpan. Then she opened the lower right-hand door, gave the tool in her hand a twist, and hooked it into the ashpan. 'Empty this twice a day,' she ordered. 'Like this.' She trotted outside, pan full of glowing embers outthrust like a fish impaled on a spear, and dumped it into a sieve over a bucket. The ashes sifted through, and the coals were thriftily returned to the fire pit.

Then, kneeling by the Rayburn's ashpan door, she pointed to a slotted circle at its base. 'See this vent? Keep it open just a bit, the fire won't burn without air from below. And the *other* damper'—she suddenly stood up and withdrew a plate at the base of the flue pipe—'must come way out if you want a hot fire. There's an indicator here'—pointing to the upper of the two left-hand doors—'that tells you how hot the oven is, and *here*'—flinging open the other left-hand door, which brought her down to her knees again—'is the warming oven. It's fine for making Melba toast and drying shoes.'

A city girl all my life, without even camping experience behind me, I must have looked as frightened as I felt. Lady Headington sought to reassure me. 'It's quite simple, really; you'll get the knack in no time. And if by chance the fire should go out don't worry. I've had an electric coil installed in the water tank. It's useful in hot weather, when you won't want a fire in the kitchen, and you'll be grateful for it when you let the Rayburn go cold to clean the flue. . . .'

'Clean the flue?' I quavered.

'That's right, I *did* neglect to mention that little odd job, didn't I? Once a month if you don't mind. Soot fires can be rather messy. The brush is on a peg in the corner. And there's stove blacking in the cupboard.'

I noted with relief that the kitchen also contained a tiny gas range. There was a small refrigerator, too, comparable to those of the 1930s in the United States, with no back on the freezing compartment; and a pantry. Behind the door was a shallow cul-de-sac in whose shadowy depths I glimpsed an ancient Hoover. An electric iron and household cleaning supplies were on a shelf. (Regrettably, I never used the stove blacking. Nor the lavender-scented bowl cleanser.)

Throughout the house I had noted an odd assortment of heaters: one or two to a room, in addition to the living-room fireplace and the two ranges in the kitchen. From Lady Headington's manner as she pointed them out, I had gathered that this was a colossal amount of equipment. It pleased her to have me recognize the fact. She had assembled so much, she said, because Americans like their rooms boiling hot.

(And don't try to tell the English anything to the contrary. You can convince them—maybe—that the streets of Chicago are moderately free of gangsters these days, or that *some* American children obey their parents, but you can never, never convince an Englishman that Americans like their rooms other than boiling hot.)

The electric heaters—I soon learned to call them electric fires— were self-explanatory, but the others baffled me. They were of enamelled steel, approximately three feet square, with neither flue nor cord. 'Oh, those are paraffin heaters,' my mentor said. 'I believe your word for the fuel they burn is kerosene. They're efficient and economical—and easy to manage, too.

'One lifts the lid . . . See? There's the reservoir. Holds a gallon. The drum is outside, the ironmonger will keep it full for you. . . . Now, to light it, you raise this wire guard, remove the cylinder, turn up the wheel on the right—it releases paraffin to the wick, you know—and set a match to the wick . . . So!' The wick was a strip of stiff webbing, and I watched in fascination as the fire crawled around it. Lady Headington continued, replacing the cylinder as she spoke, 'Now, when the dome on the cylinder glows red, the wheel should be turned down again. That's all there is to it; very simple, once you get the knack. . . . Flames? Oh, so there are. A bit too much paraffin, I dare say.' She spun the wheel lower, then, as an afterthought, remarked, 'By the way, watch the wicks. If they aren't trimmed properly or replaced as needed, you'll be bothered by smoke.'

Well, I told myself, *at least the paraffin heaters are smaller than the Rayburn. Perhaps they'll be easier to subdue.*

Lady Headington gave us lunch, but hurried us through. 'Thursday is early closing,' she said, 'and if you wish to lay on supplies we must get to the shops before one.' The butcher shops shut their doors on Monday and Saturday afternoons, in addition, she told us; and the wine merchant was open (for the purchase of spirits) only during 'hours', which I later found out meant during the same hours the pubs were open.

The rain had stopped, but the air was heavy with moisture and the sky was still grey. Umbrellas in hand, we set out— skirting puddles, hopping over curbside rivulets, and dodging the chestnut trees that hung dripping heads over garden walls. First we went to Mrs Bond's shop at the bottom—I would have said, 'at the end'— of the street, for the few staple groceries I knew I'd need immediately. At Berry's, the bakery, I bought a small round loaf of bread, receiving it with a piece of thin paper loosely wrapped around part of it. At Murchison's the Heading-ton Greengrocer, I added newspaper-wrapped potatoes, carrots, and a limp head of lettuce to the bundles in Red's arms.

Our final stop was H. E. Weaver's Quality Meats, and there I made a mistake. Walking along, I had made a quick calculation as to what might be the simplest menu to prepare, and I had answered myself: a good Irish stew. So I asked Mr Weaver for 'a pound of beef for stew,' expecting the succulent squares of chuck that the same request would have produced at home. I don't know what he gave me, because I never ordered it again. . . . But I'm getting ahead of my story.

I had finished unpacking our suitcases when, in the late after-noon, George arrived. He had picked up the car we had ordered before we left home, and had driven down from London. (Oxford is actually north of London, but since in England one always goes up to the capital, travel in the reverse direction *has* to be down.) I had not noticed upon arrival that there was a pub across the street, and now the curb in front of it was solid with parked cars. Consequently George had to back and fill for ten minutes before he was able to get our car into the narrow garage. Later on he refined his system of garaging so the car slid in like a sausage into a casing; sometimes, in fact, he positioned it so smoothly that one could open the doors on *either* side. But that accomplishment was still in the future, and he therefore entered his new English home for the first time tired and cross.

Determined not to burden him further, I turned Pollyanna as I showed him around the house, Red drifting silently behind us. But George reads me clearly; he kept saying, 'Well. now, isn't that nice?' in much too hearty a manner as I called his attention to the bouquets, and to the ship's clock; to the big kitchen table, and to the door that opened off the dining-room into the garden; to the simplicity of the decoration in our bedroom, and the fine big closet Lady Headington had had newly built into a corner there. His only reference to the living-room was oblique: 'I guess we're going to have to learn to keep our elbows in, eh?'

Meanwhile, renewed rain pattered gently onto the plastic roof of the solarium and gurgled down the spout just outside the kitchen door, and the stew bubbled along on the top of the Rayburn. While I set the table with my gleaming college silver, George essayed a fire in the living-room fireplace. He's a master fire builder at home, but in California one burns wood; and now he was using coal. He tried paper spills, then live embers from the Rayburn, much pumping of the bellows, and finally a dollop of paraffin. (*George*, who normally considers the application of fire-lighting fluid to be as shocking a practice as dousing a steak with catsup!) But the fire wouldn't catch. He cursed it while I cursed the stew. After four hours of cooking a fork still wouldn't penetrate the meat.

At 8.30 I said, 'Let's eat it. If we cut it into small enough pieces, we won't even have to chew it.' I *did* chew one piece of mine to see what it tasted like, and it didn't have any taste.

Red, sensing my distress and doing his best to relieve it, said, 'The potatoes are awfully good, Mom.'

'I'm glad you like them,' I said with savage politeness, and burst into tears.

I lay awake for quite a time that night, listening to the rain on the roof and looking at the pattern thrown on the bedroom ceiling by the lamp across the street. I thought about the stew. *Tomorrow's dinner will be good*, I promised myself, and wondered whether I'd be satisfied to be just a housewife, after having had a paying job for all those years. I said a little prayer for Redmond's happiness in his new school, and for the success of George's lectures. *They say that Oxford undergraduates refuse to attend lectures. What if no one comes?* I let my thoughts drift back to the electric range in my California kitchen, and to the furnace we lit by pressing a button, and to the big living-room in our Spanish-style house, with its unadorned white plaster walls and its wide open spaces of rug and its quietness of shape and colour. *Now, that's enough of that,* I told myself. *You're not going to be homesick, ever again.* The ship's clock downstairs struck eight bells, and the street lamp across the way dimmed out, and before long I fell asleep.

Chapter 2

WE AWAKENED to a blue and gold world. The air was so clear it made us blink, even looking at it from indoors—and who could stay indoors on a morning like this one? Breakfast could wait; out we went.

There ahead of us was a pretty little grey and white bird splashing about in the bird bath in the centre of the gravelled side yard; whenever he flicked his wings, he stirred up a teacup-sized tempest of droplets and set them flying in shining parabolas into space. Atop the handsome old stone wall that bordered the yard sat a mammoth black cat with topaz eyes, staring gravely at the bird. And in front of the gate that opened into the garden there was a turtle that seemed to be smiling and wagging his tail. This was not such a silly notion, as it turned out, for the turtle was a neighbour's house pet, was very fond of paying social calls in the neighbourhood, and in due course became rather a nuisance. But on that first morning in Oxford the turtle and the cat and the bird gave us the feeling that Peter Rabbit and his friends had turned out to welcome us.

The garden behind the gate was over a hundred feet deep, with lush turf; there was a bed bright with dahlias and daisies in the foreground and a vegetable garden in the rear. There, too, were five apple trees, one as gnarled and twisted as a Monterey cypress, and at their feet some rosy windfalls glimmered.

George, reared on a Nebraska farm, estimated the coming harvest. 'Gee, honey, there must be three or four bushels on those trees. Think of the apple pies you can make.'

This was a gibe, for my failures with pie crust were family legend, but I let it pass. 'Heavens,' I said, 'even if we get 'em picked, wherever are we going to *keep* them?'

'Over there,' George replied, pointing to a storage shed he had spotted at one side of the garden, half hidden in a tangle of vines. Lady Headington must have used it for the same purpose, for it contained paper-covered shelves that gave off a faint fruity odour. Over the door we noted a fading stencilled name 'BLAZE'; the next day, when we met our part-time gardener, he told us that Blaze was an 'orse the previous hoccupants of the 'ouse 'ad 'ad.

The fire in the Rayburn had gone out— we had forgotten to stoke and bank it the night before—but in this morning's mood we didn't care. While George rebuilt it, I set about frying bacon and eggs on the little gas range. It was like those one sometimes sees in American Pullman kitchenettes, except that its oven was not equipped with jets for broiling. Instead, they lay in two rows directly below the top burners, in a six-inch cavity between the burners and the drip tray. Into this cavity one could insert a grill pan just big enough for three chops or four slices of bread. I never had any trouble broiling chops, because I could hear them sputtering, but since I couldn't see the bread and forgot about it, the toast we ate in England was usually burned. (Unless we ate it away from home; then it was pale tan and cold. English housewives toast it before they start the coffee, then carefully set it off to one side to cool to proper temperature for eating.)

The reason I burned the toast that first morning was that the mailman and the milkman arrived together—the mailman on a bicycle, which he parked at the curb as he peeled two letters off the bundle in his hand, and the milkman in a gleaming white truck labelled 'Job's Dairy'. Would we be wanting him to serve us regularly?

'Oh yes,' I said. 'We'll need a quart of homogenized milk . . .'

'It doesn't come homogenized, madam. The Guernsey is very nice.'

'Fine. A quart of Guernsey, then . . .'

'It doesn't come in quarts, madam. Just pints.'

'Fine. Two pints, then. And perhaps some half 'n' half, or the equivalent? In the States, we like it for cereal. It's half milk and half cream, homogen—oh! Well, perhaps you'd better leave another pint, then. We'll use the top milk.'

British immigration officials had been pleasant but firm, and our passports were clearly stamped: 'Permitted to land at Liverpool on 16th September on condition that the holder does not remain in the United Kingdom longer than twelve months, and registers at once with the police.' The 'at once' had been stressed, so as soon as the fire in the Rayburn was crackling away again, and the breakfast dishes were dried, we gathered up a street map and the photos of ourselves that we had been told to bring, and set out for Oxford police station.

Headington is two miles from the city centre, and on higher ground. The street we followed descends the hill through a deep cut over which the tree tops join; at that time of year driving through it is like tunnelling through a green cavern. At the bottom lies a flat plain that is called The Plain, and on the left we noted a sweep of incredibly green meadow in which several placid horses were grazing. I thought, *How lovely. And how strange I didn't see this yesterday when the taxi brought us up from the station.* The meadow was particularly restful to the eyes because it was bordered on all sides by ugly row houses of red brick.

The street, wide up to this point, suddenly narrowed; and as suddenly filled. Cars and buses seemed to spew into it from a series of side streets, and we inched along until a bend brought us face to face with a roundabout (a traffic circle; the British prefer them to intersections controlled by traffic lights). It resembled a runaway carousel, and I caught my breath. But George, thanks to his drive from London on the previous day, was a veteran, and he tackled the maelstrom ahead of us with cheer and confidence.

'There's no right of way at these,' he explained, his head swivelling and his foot ready on the gas pedal. 'The trick is to cut in front of the first driver that hesitates. A good time to catch 'em is when they're shifting gears . . . So!' He shot into the stream like a salmon in springtime. I would have congratulated him, and he would have congratulated himself, had we not just then found ourselves facing one of Oxford's most beautiful landmarks—the stone bridge that spans the Cherwell River, Magdalen (pronounced 'Maudlin') College, and its magnificent fifteenth-century tower.

Solidly set, strong and simple, the tower's lower windows are narrow and unornamented, and its tawny stones are rough in texture. But slenderness gives it a vigorous upward thrust, and heaven touches it as it rises. The upper windows are high and elegantly arched, the stone is smooth, there is ornamental fretwork and gallery around the belfry, and at the summit a series of feathery pinnacles fling themselves into the sky. In its frame of trees, sky, and water, and despite the vitality of the tower itself, the view across Magdalen Bridge is a tranquil one. There is a soothing spaciousness about it that we came to appreciate even more fully as we discovered its rarity in modern Oxford.

After we had crossed the bridge, the city closed in. Oh, High Street curved on sweetly enough—past the classic cupola of Queen's College, the lovely lace-frilled St Mary the Virgin Church, and the austere spire of All Saints—but on that day we couldn't see the beauties that lie beyond the curbs because we didn't dare lengthen our focus beyond a car's length. There is a chronic traffic tangle on this street, since it leads to the Carfax, the only real intersection in Oxford, the one place where north-south and east-west traffic meet; but on the day of our baptism we had made the mistake of tackling the town during the morning rush hour, and vehicles were approaching this intersection in a spirit of no quarter given, none expected. The street was raucous with the roar of motors, and a bluish haze born of exhaust smoke eddied about the patient queues of people at the bus stops. No sleepy university town, this; it was like travelling on a cross-town street in Manhattan at high noon. When George finally managed the necessary left turn at the Carfax and a short run south on St Aldate's Street brought us to the police station, we felt as if we'd found sanctuary.

Incidentally, it's an odd feeling to be registered as an alien, if up to that moment in your experience *other* people have always been the aliens.

The formality completed, George proposed that we go to see Balliol. To get there seemed simple enough: we'd retrace our rout on St Aldate's, but instead of turning toward Headington at the Carfax we'd go straight ahead to Broad Street. We noted a puzzling detail, however: although the street we'd be following on the other side of the Carfax appeared to be a direct continuation of the one we were on, it had a different name— Cornmarket Street.

Red, looking at the map over George's shoulder, made a belated discovery. 'High Street quits at the Carfax too,' he said. 'On the other side it's called Queen Street. And look: it forks almost right away, but one fork is called New Road and the other is Castle Street.'

'Yes, that's right,' George said, having scanned the entire map. 'Street names change at each intersection. Now I understand why Peters'—an Englishman recently in residence in California —'thought it worth mentioning that he drove west on Sunset Boulevard for twenty miles and it was *still* Sunset Boulevard.' 'I remember too that he was shocked by the house numbers in five figures,' I recalled. 'Now I see why.'

We crawled north on Cornmarket Street, past the musty Victorian façades of food stores and bakeries, a bank and some dress shops, and then found ourselves stalled between the twentieth century and the tenth. The twentieth, on the left, was an enormous, shiny, glass-fronted, fluorescent-lit Woolworth's that people were entering and leaving like bees at a hive. The tenth century, ahead on the right, was a rubble tower of modest height, as rough as Woolworth's was slick. Red checked the guidebook: 'One of the few remaining examples of Saxon architecture in the city . . . Gaunt, unadorned, with round-headed windows, good for shooting from with a bow. . . .. It was here that the North Gate, which included a prison called the Bocardo, spanned the street. . . . The inmates used to let down a greasy old hat and cry to passers-by, "Pity the Bocardo birds!" ' '

I tried to visualize the street as it might have looked with a gate and watch tower from which archers showered foes with arrows, and where tenderhearted townsmen tossed a few pence to the poor birds in the Bocardo, but Woolworth's and the autos all around us kept getting in the way. Nor, as we passed the tower, was it easy to banish the packed-tight buildings on its other side and replace them with either the earth embankment of William the Conqueror's day or with the stone wall that enclosed the city about the time King John had signed the Magna Carta at Runnymede. However, it *was* easy to locate the broad ditch that had protected both of these walls. We parked in the middle of it. It had been filled in, becoming a broad street. Balliol College fronted on Broad Street.

Our first view of Balliol was disappointing. It was just a chain of dirty, grey stone buildings with a Scottish baronial tower on one end, at the base of which was a door that looked as small as a mousehole. No matter; we had been told that the Oxford colleges hide their beauties, and we started across the street toward it. That's when I noticed a brick cross set into the cobbled street, flush with its surface. 'I wonder what it means?' I mused. 'That's easy,' Red said. 'Something religious happened here.' 'Let's be sure to look it up in the guidebook later,' I told him. Stepping through the little door of the college, we found ourselves in a stone foyer. The walls on one side were hidden by stacks of trunks and boxes, heralding the return of undergraduates who would soon be arriving for the fall term. A doorway on the right led into what could only be the porter's lodge. There were pigeonholes for mail, a telephone booth, a counter, and behind it a tidy little man in sober black.

But we barely glanced at him, because standing there too was a man with bushy iron-grey eyebrows and a wild mane of hair that almost reached the collar of his tweed jacket. There were leather patches on the elbows of his jacket; his trousers had gentle bags that were quite independent of the current position of his own knees; and an umbrella as formidable in size as a medieval broadsword hung over one forearm. I thought, a *don at last!* He shuffled through the mail in one of the pigeonholes, withdrew a notice, shifted the umbrella to his right hand, and walked passed us as unseeingly as if there had been no one there. Surely this had to be a don. I was enchanted.

Then George heard his name called. Stepping through the mousehole was a man whose appearance and manner were so commonplace that I didn't peg him as a don, too—although he was in fact equally one with the other. Romantic notions die hard, and I felt cheated when I finally got it through my head that don is simply a contraction of 'dominus' and is the Oxford title for anyone who teaches at the university. A don may or—more likely—may not look as if he's gotten up for a fancy-dress ball.

'Why, it's Roger Mackenzie!' George exclaimed, pumping the newcomer's hand. 'Honey, I first knew Roger at Harvard. He's visited the United States often, and gave a fine seminar at Caltech just last spring. Roger, are you a Fellow of Balliol?' Roger was; and I could see George relax. How pleasant to know already one of his future associates.

'Have you been here long?' Roger inquired, and we told him that this was our initial visit to the college, and that we had arrived just before he had. 'Well, let me show you round,' he said, and we gratefully followed him.

Beyond the entry lay a grassy quadrangle, its four sides formed by stern, stone buildings that Roger identified as the library, the chapel, undergraduates' rooms, and offices. The windows had an icy stare. We ducked through a narrow passageway and into the chapel, a walnut-panelled room with lots of stained glass, a silver altar, and a gleaming brass lectern. Somehow it looked more like an authentic copy of something than the real McCoy; and I found out later why this was so. It was so heavily restored in the nineteenth century that nothing remains of the original chapel except a few bits of fourteenth- and seventeenth-century glass that have been preserved in the modern windows.

But through another narrow passageway a little jewel awaited us : the Fellows' Garden, a low-walled enclosure with benches and flowers and turf so well tended it had the unreal look of stage grass. As I took a step forward into it, Roger hastily said, 'I'm sorry. It's the *Fellows'* Garden.' He paused discreetly, but I still looked blank. 'For their exclusive use,' he continued. 'Others don't—er—enter.'

However, others do enter the big quadrangle behind it, and it was a lovely sight. Fleecy puffs of cloud now speckled the brilliant blue of the sky, the smooth lawns sparkled in sun, and there was enough wind to set the branches of the lofty elms and chestnuts dancing. At the far end of this garden was the dining-hall, and Roger led us up the stairs to look in.

Almost three stories high, the huge room was dusky even on this bright day. The stone walls and Jacobean oak panelling blotted up the small amount of light admitted by the Gothic windows, and the heavy beams arching across the ceiling were swallowed in shadow. Small sections of each window were open, but each was masked by a wide-grid screen—a modern touch that struck me as odd, and I said so.

'Oh, but they're necessary to keep the birds out,' Roger said. 'Great numbers of sparrows used to perch on those beams, and it was sometimes unpleasant for the diners at table below . . . .'

I could imagine.

'. . . because the birds liked to take dust baths up there, and they did dislodge rather a lot of debris.'

The tables were long and narrow, three columns of them, each with benches, and they were set at right angles to a dais that spanned one end of the hall.

'That's High Table,' Roger explained. 'Where the Fellows sit.'
Then, speaking directly to George, 'I hope you will join us often;
we've a good chef and a fine cellar.'

George grinned at me. 'Men only, honey.'

I said, 'All the time? Don't you even have Ladies' Night, or
something of that sort?'

Roger smiled. 'No, I'm afraid it's an unbreakable rule that
women may not dine in Hall during term. We were never a
college for the clergy, like Merton, nor supported by a religious
order, like Worcester, but there is a monkish residum at *all* the
colleges. There was a time, you know, when Fellows were supposed to be in orders, and it wasn't until late in the nineteenth
century that we were allowed to marry.'

As he talked, we had been sauntering around the hall, glancing
at the portraits that studded the oak wainscot, and at this point
Roger broke off his discourse and pointed to one. 'John Wycliffe.
He was Master here.'

'Wycliffe the Bible translator?' I asked.

'Yes, but that was afterwards. He was Master of Balliol around
1360.' (How easily he said, '1360'; as if it were just last week.)

'And up there is the Founder, John de Balliol, and his wife,'
Roger continued, gesturing toward a pair of portraits hidden in
the gloom. 'He was a North Country baron who started the
college for the support of sixteen poor scholars. It was a penance
laid on him in 1260 or so by the Bishop of Durham. I don't
know what he had done to deserve it.'

'But what I don't understand,' I said as we left the hall and
stood gazing down at the big quadrangle and the multi-coloured
brick tower beside the chapel, 'is why, if the college is so old, it
looks so, well, *Victorian*.'

Roger chuckled. 'Most of the buildings *are* Victorian. They
replaced old ones or were given during our great period of growth
in the nineteenth century. People like Southey and Swinburne
and Matthew Arnold—and the great Master, Jowett—made us
famous. Now we're said to have the best brains and the worst
food in Oxford.'

'I thought you said the chef is good,' George reminded him.

'He is,' Roger replied. 'There's a twenty-year time lag on this
sort of thing.'

We were proceeding along a stone-flagged passageway when I

stumbled and steadied myself by reaching out toward the wall. My hand came to rest on wood, and I turned to look. Hung against the wall was a very heavy and seemingly ancient door, so black it appeared to be charred.

'That used to be one of the college gates, and it *is* charred,' Roger responded to my query. 'It got scorched when Archbishop Cranmer was burned at the stake in the ditch that used to run along in front of the college; it's Broad Street now.'

'The cross in the street!' Red exclaimed.

'Oh, you noticed it?' Roger replied. 'Yes, there. Did you also notice the Saxon tower on Cornmarket before you turned into the Broad? In the sixteenth century it was used as a prison. They say that when Latimer and Ridley—they died a year before Cranmer, in 1555—were put to the stake, the archbishop was brought to the top of the tower so he could see what was in store for him. Rather gruesome, what?'

'But the cross is quite some distance from the present entrance,' I demurred.

'Well, it was quite a fire,' Roger answered. 'I don't know how true this story is, but I've been told that the wood was characteristically so damp that condemned heretics didn't so much burn at the stake as slowly roast to death.'

I swallowed painfully.

'So it was the humane custom in those pre-Elizabethan days to allow the victim to buy gunpowder and secrete it on his body. But Cranmer is said to have refused the comfort, if one could call it that, of death by explosion; and he died so slowly and so agonizingly that someone finally took pity on him and tossed a bucket of pitch on the fire. That's why it blazed up fiercely enough to scorch the gates of the college.'

'The good old days,' George murmured.

'A hard lot, our forebears,' Roger agreed.

Then he took us to the west door of the college and pointed out, on St Giles' Street, a slim grey stone spire as richly embellished as a wedding cake and approximately twenty-five feet high.

'The Martyrs' Memorial,' Roger explained. 'It was put up in the 1840s. Read the inscription sometime, it's rather nice. "To the glory of God, and in grateful commemoration of His servants, Thomas Cranmer, Nicholas Ridley, and Hugh Latimer, Prelates of the Church of England, who near this spot yielded their bodies

to be burned." Splendid rolling rhythm, don't you agree?
'Until quite recently, to climb the Martyrs' Memorial was a favourite undergraduate sport, but they can be sent down—you'd say "expelled"—for it now, so they save their strength for week-end visits to Cambridge, or for holidays on Snowdon.'

'What makes Oxford so confusing,' I said at breakfast the next morning, 'is that the chronology is so mixed up. You have to keep hopping from the Reformation to the Norman Conquest to the Industrial Revolution, and at the same time you're signing an application for a telephone or buying some frozen peas for dinner.'

George grinned. 'What did you expect? Another Williams-burg, with people all dressed up in hoop skirts?'

'Well, it would certainly be easier on a tourist,' I rejoined.

'You're the one who kept talking about living history,' Red reminded me.

'And how being here would deepen our understanding of our own culture,' George added.

'Oh, quit needling me.' But they were right: I'd had a worse case of nostalgia for the homeland than either of them. Not that Britain was in any physical sense a homeland to any of us, except way back, when the Bothwells and Joneses and McClures on my family tree, and the Albros and Spaldings on George's, had emigrated to the United States from their various corners of the British Isles. But there was French and German blood in us, too, and we had no family ties to anybody outside the United States, so the only explanation for my feeling that we were coming home to England was sentiment.

A good many Americans feel so, even if their names are Martinez or Stepanek. I dare say it's because we hear about the Pilgrim Fathers so often and from such a tender age that by the time we find out that there were Dutchmen in New York and Spaniards in St Augustine we think of them as foreign inter-lopers. Through school, almost the only non-native literature to which we are exposed is English, and almost the only history we study, after our own, is Western European. And somehow the names and scenes that linger, hazy with romance and bright with derring-do are Robin Hood and Sherlock Holmes and Nelson dying on the quarterdeck. Good Queen Bess was on the throne in ... 1066? 1215? 1588? Anyway, *she's* the one for whom Raleigh spread his cape. Eliza's rain stays mainly on the plain. And Burma is ... ? Oh yes, Burma is where the dawn comes up like thunder out of China 'cross the bay. God bless us, every one!

Out of such stuff—if it has turned one into an Anglophile—has evolved an expectation that the modern Englishman will be a paragon of the civilized virtues, his character as stout as Churchill's, his manner as suave as the Schweppesman's. Since the English themselves rather agree with this view, it is no wonder that so many Americans go to England feeling like raw colonials—even Americans as basically sensible as the three of us.

We knew, because we already knew some Englishmen, that they come in assorted sizes, shapes, and casts of mind, and that stereotypes are treacherous. But emotional attitudes lie deep. It was at this time, too, that our own and other periodicals were levelling a drumfire of criticism at Americans abroad. We are boastful, loud, and arrogant, they told us. We equate a high degree of civilisation with how well the plumbing works. American women are immodest. American men are Milquetoasts. And our young are savages. This is no more true than that all Englishmen like well-done beef, ride to hounds, or have stiff upper lips, but it had its impact on George and Red and me. Just below the surface of my mind was a resolve not to be bossy in public or shrill in speech. George, despite the fact that he is a distinguished scientist and teacher, was awed by the reputation of Oxford, and fearful that he wouldn't measure up. Red doesn't wear his heart on his sleeve, but I had noticed a tightening of the mouth and a squaring of the jaw whenever his new school was mentioned, and I think he expected the boys to have a parade-ground bearing and tea-party manners, and the teachers to be as cold as fish.

It's hard now to recapture the feeling of timidity with which we three set out that morning to meet the headmaster of Magdalen College School, to which Red had been provisionally (we *thought;* it had never been said in so many words) accepted. Although we had been corresponding with the Master for almost a year, if he didn't now like our accents of the cut of Red's jib, he could still reject the boy.

An Oxford friend had recommended the school; the Master had sent its entrance exam to Red's 'headmaster' at his Pasadena

junior high school; and the whole administrative staff plus ourselves had been torn between laughter and tears as we had
studied it. Red had been nearly fourteen then, in the ninth grade,
and was just starting Latin and algebra. Yet the exam, which
English boys take at thirteen, required knowledge of both Latin
and French, algebra *and* geometry, and there was even a section
to test his familiarity with Scripture. It was obvious that he
couldn't pass it. Since we had already read in the school catalogue
that 'boys of 11 or less at the time of entry are not expected to
show knowledge of Latin, French, Algebra, or Geometry, but
will have an opportunity of doing so,' we accepted as fact that
our young product of the American public schools was far, far
behind his contemporaries in England.

Besides, the Sputniks had gone up just a few months earlier,
and Americans were reeling with shock—including me, who
should have known better. My newspaper specialty for many
years had been to report news of education. I'd been in so many
schools I was frequently taken for a teacher, and I knew perfectly well that those members of our citizenry who were attacking our schools as failures had obviously not been near one lately.
Nevertheless, if one hears often that American children are
always put back a year or two in England, or that the academic
standards of English schools are much higher than those of
American schools, or that discipline is much tougher and
grading much more objective, it's hard to believe.

The Master of Magdalen College School had told us that
foreign boys need not pass the entrance exam, and together we
had outlined a programme of private study to prepare Red for his
English year. In addition to the Latin he was taking at school,
he had been privately tutored in French. And as soon as summer
vacation began, he did a cram course in geometry, and extended
his acquaintance with Caesar and the subjunctive. So here he
was in Oxford, ready or not, and there we were descending
Headington hill in dappled sunlight, and in a very few minutes
we found ourselves at the door of a monstrous Victorian mansion
across the bridge from Magdalen College.

The school takes boys from nine to eighteen, many of the
younger ones on musical scholarships. It is supported in part by
the college across the way, in order to have a handy supply of
choirboys for its chapel services; in fact, one of the tourist

attractions of Oxford is to watch the choristers, in pint-sized caps and gowns, trotting across the bridge for Evensong. But Red is no singer, so he was to enrol—if they'd have him—as a paying student.

When our ring was answered, we were led through a dim hallway into a dim study. There the Master, a dim silhouette against what light there was, greeted us. A short, greying man with a bristly moustache, a soft voice, and a kindly manner (whom had I been expecting? Wackford Squeers?), he asked Red some questions about his background in maths and science, and we all made small talk. Had our journey from the States been pleasant? Yes, very. We had accommodations in Oxford? Oh yes—a nice little house in Headington. Professor Beadle would be lecturing at the university? He was going to try. He was scheduled to give two series of lectures on biochemical genetics. How interesting. (We learned later that the Master is a Latin scholar and a historian, so he *was* being polite). Finally George asked a question: How much was the tuition?

The Master paused and reflected. Then: 'I'm not certain, I believe it was to have been increased this term. Let me inquire of the secretary.' He excused himself and left the room; and we eyed his departing back respectfully. In as much as Mr Bennett at Balliol had been unable to tell George at what intervals he would be paid, I was now convinced that English academic people dwell in a much more rarified spiritual world than we dollar-conscious Americans.

Outdoors again, the interview over, Red asked, 'Did he accept me, Pop?'

George replied, 'In the absence of a negative, we'll assume a positive. I guess you're in, boy.'

So we went shopping for school clothes.

The school outfitter occupied a plain little shop with an oriental rug on the floor. The salesman spread out an impressive—and impressively priced—array of undershirts, underpants, knee-high wool socks, grey Viyella shirts, red-striped black ties, grey worsted trousers, red-bound black blazers, visored caps, red-bordered black Rugby socks, navy twill shorts and red Rugby shirts, a white wool sweater that looked good enough for the Duke of Edinburgh, grey Shetland sweaters, a mackintosh, and a heavy duffle coat. We bought most of it.

The only items that were compulsory, he told us, were the cap and school tie, but most of the boys wore the blazer, too. Both it and the cap were ornamented with a lily embroidered in white. This symbol derives from the school motto, 'Sicut Lilium', which derives from the lilies of Magdalen College. They in turn derive from the lilies of Eton College, which were borrowed in 1458 by William Waynflete, Lord Chancellor of England and Bishop of Winchester, when he founded Magdalen College. I don't know where Eton got the lilies, and am willing to stop at 1458. It is impressive enough to know that Red's school was founded soon after the college from which it takes its name, and that on the day Columbus set sail for the Indies pupils at Magdalen College School were intoning their Latin lessons in a building extant.

Red was rather taken with himself in his new uniform. I too considered it an improvement over the blue jeans and cotton sports shirts he had been wearing at his Pasadena school. 'But, Mom,' he cautioned, 'don't let the word get back home that I'm going to a school whose motto is "Pure as a Lily".'

As I watched the salesman total the bill, I said to myself that it was just because I was new in England that English money was incomprehensible, and that I'd get the hang of it in no time. This was a false prophecy; I never did. Not that it was difficult to shift from dollars to pounds as the basic unit, or to decide whether a given item was a good buy at its price. An experienced shopper can do *that* whether the medium of exchange is clamshells or coins.

My basic trouble was that I never learned to count my change. I'd repeat like a litany—'Twelve pence in a shilling, twenty shillings in a pound'—and find myself staring helplessly at a fistful of huge copper pennies, silver sixpences, yellow three-pences, and those look-a-likes, the two-shilling piece and the half-crown. I couldn't even pronounce them easily. Hardly ever did I go to the post office without eavesdropping in admiration as someone asked for a tuppence-ha'penny and two thr'p'ny stamps, and ten bob's worth of savings stamps.

A tanner is a sixpence, a bob is a shilling, a quid is a pound, and a guinea *isn't*. It would be worth twenty-one shillings if it existed; or maybe it does, in a ghostly way, because prices of merchandise or services with snob appeal (i.e., Red's white sweater) are quoted in guineas. But whenever one pays a five-guinea bill by check—by cheque, I mean— it is written as five pounds, five shillings.

Loaded with bundles of clothing for Red, we drove back up Headington hill and shopped for the house. I was still, of course, in the sampling stage, getting acquainted with shopkeepers and stocks by trying them all.

In a country where cookies and crackers have to be bought as biscuits, where lemons are advertised as a condiment for pancakes and chili sauce is chutney, where tapioca is sago and is ground as fine as corn meal—speaking of which, there isn't any, the hopefully bought box of corn *flour* turning out to be corn-*starch*—where, in short, so many foodstuffs come in unfamiliar shapes and textures it was surprising to meet so many old friends: Heinz, and Birds Eye, Chase & Sanborn, Kleenex, Dreft, and Lux. These familiar brand names gave me a false sense of security, for the products that bear these names are blended for English tastes. The tomato juice was spicier and the coffee was more bitter than we were accustomed to, and even a Betty Crocker cake mix—her English name is Mary Baker—came from the oven much drier and more crumbly than in the United States.

But it was fun to buy and try, and that particular day's shopping spree yielded a treasure—a package of fruit gelatine that American grocers would do well to copy. Any woman who has tried to make up half a recipe of powdered fruit gelatine—what's half of three ounces translated into standard measuring spoons?—will appreciate my delight when I opened my first English package of the stuff and found a rubbery block of gum, scored in squares. Half the squares equal half the recipe: hail Britannia!

In addition to foodstuffs my shopping list that day included waxed paper, dishcloths, thumbtacks, and a couple of frogs for the bouquets I hoped to keep in the house. Since we had decided to plant a small flower bed in front of the wall outside the kitchen window, George wanted spring bulbs, and some kindling wood for both the fireplace and the Rayburn. We were having a tough time keeping either one lit.

We found the bulbs at a florist's shop, and they were so big, beautiful, and cheap that George got drunk with enthusiasm and bought ten dozen. My request for frogs produced, first, a blank look from the salesgirl; second, when the function of frogs was explained, a ball of chicken wire called maizie; and third, a politely suppressed but unmistakable giggle. What odd names Americans give to ordinary objects!

The kindling turned up at the ironmonger's, where it was packaged as a neat little bundle of thin six-inch-long sticks and was called firewood. Because there were so many hardware items on display I asked for the thumbtacks here, and ran into another language barrier. 'They're metal,' I said, 'with broad flat heads and sharp points. I want them to fix some oilcloth to a shelf over my sink. . . . Oh? *Drawing pins?* Well, think of that. And I'll find them at the stationer's? Thank you.'

At the stationer's I also found the waxed (that is, 'greaseproof') paper, but I never repeated the purchase. The stuff came in flat sheets rather than on rolls and was so stiff it crackled like parchment. As for the rest of my list, dishcloths seemed to be nonexistent in England. Pot holders too. I later imported some of both. The English housewife grabs a towel or the corner of her apron and wads it around her skillet handle.

That afternoon, as George was planting the bulbs, we had our first caller: Kitty Turnbull. A mutual friend had written her to look in on us, and since Kitty is both dutiful and curious, here she was—a modish young woman, her fair hair dressed in a bouffant Paris style, her tweeds faultless, her smile of greeting echoed in her eyes, her voice the bird song that makes the speech of the cultivated English woman so beguiling.

She had brought us a jar of marmalade and a marrow—which is a kind of giant zucchini—from her garden, and I gave her a glass of sherry. (I was too timid to propose tea, what if I forgot to heat the pot?) Later, when we took her on a tour of the place, she nodded her head in the direction of the side yard and remarked, 'Isn't that *like* Americans, though! Improving the place, and you're only going to be here a year!'

I cooked the marrow for dinner, It tasted like wax, and the ice cream I'd bought the day before had the consistency of gravy when I took it out of the ice tray. But there were no tears that night. No house is strange once you've opened its door to a friend. No soil is alien once you've planted bulbs.

Chapter 3

'WHAT ARE WE doing today?' George asked the next morning, 'Picking apples. Name tapes have to be sewn on all of Red's school clothes. And shouldn't you go to the lab and let them know you're here?'

'Let's go on a trip, instead. I'd kind of like to see Stonehenge.'

We got back three days later. We had travelled on some terrifying highways and beautiful byways, had fallen in love with pagan Britain and pub signs, had eaten incredibly uninteresting food at amazingly cheap and well-run hotels—and, in sum, had begun to understand why people who emigrate from England ever afterward yearn for it.

Oxford, fifty miles west and slightly north of London, lies in the centre of the plain where the Thames rises. The nearby landscape is green and watery, and the fields flow away from the streams in long, undulating slopes. None is without a stand of splendid trees—linden or beech, elm or oak. Ringing the plain on the south and the west is open, windy country that rises into those uplands the English call downs. Sometimes one sees flocks of sheep idling along on the lower slopes, and leggy white pigs rooting around the trees. It was this country we explored, our route swinging across Oxfordshire into Wiltshire and down into Somerset, skirting the Bristol Channel, as far as Wells.

Before the Roman came to Rye or out to Severn strode,
The rolling English drunkard made the rolling English road.

. . . and there hasn't been any compelling reason for straightening it, so it still meanders through the countryside like a lazy river, its channels marked by hedges or windrows of saplings. There are surprises around each bend, like trinkets tumbling from one of those coiled-paper balls that children love to unwind: a thatched-roof cottage of Cotswold stone, salvia burning bright at its doorstep; a sweep of flatland supine under a canopy of rolling cloud; a squat grey church in a distant valley, its spire poking a supplicating finger above a smother of trees. These little panoramas flash into view and vanish as swiftly as if they'd been shaken out of a kaleidoscope, and we found them utterly enchanting.

We paid more attention to the landscape than to the road— at first. Then we learned that the surprise just around the bend might equally well be a lorry loaded with brick. It would come panting toward us up a grade, a big black sedan trapped in its wake. As we'd come in view of each other, the black sedan would pull out to pass—and do so, gravel spurting behind its wheels, while George swerved, braked, and cursed. 'The fool! The damn' fool! He crossed the double centre line!' Indeed he did. British drivers cross the centre line as gaily as if they were winding a Maypole from Brampton to Bournemouth. The only English road more treacherous that the commonplace two-lane road is the 'modern' three-lane highway. Motorists contest the right to use the centre lane as ferociously as if the drivers were jousting in a medieval tourney—minus the chivalry.

The British death rate per miles travelled by car was publicized while we were in England as almost 70 per cent higher than in the United States. The reason was obvious: only recently have great numbers of Britons been able to afford cars, and the highways are flooded with motorists who haven't yet come to grips with the fact that survival depends on driver discipline. They fail to signal; they park on the road on blind curves; they maintain an erratic pace. They scared the daylights out of us. George's reaction was to avoid all main roads—which is a good idea anyway if you're not in a hurry, the virtues of shun-piking being self-evident—but my reaction was to avoid driving altogether. In fact that first jaunt of ours made such an imprint on me that I turned frail and timid, and never afterward drove the car in England.

English acquaintances who know the United States were astounded when they learned that I refused to drive. 'But you drive at home, don't you?' one inquired.

'Yes, of course I do.'

'On the—er—freeways?'

'Yes.'

'Traffic jams moving at sixty-five miles per hour, that's what they are. Make you nervous?'

'Not particularly.'

'Well'—here came the trump card—'the English drive *much* slower.'

So they do. That was one of the reasons for my nervousness. Many vehicles go so slowly they invite foolhardy behaviour by the drivers they inconvenience. I had the misfortune to be behind the wheel on a stretch of road near Swindon, when we came upon a very small youngster riding a very large bicycle up a hill. The road was a narrow slot between high and thorny hedges. To attempt to pass would have been utter folly, so I shifted to lowest gear and we crept uphill at the cyclist's pace. As he approached the crest, the child—despite manful exertions—began to wobble. Watching him was a nightmare in slow motion. But it was mercifully brief. Suddenly his front wheel yawed wildly, and he toppled into the dust. Fast on his feet, he was, too; back on his bike and under way before I'd gotten our stalled engine going again.

George's nerves, however, were equal to such wear and tear, and when there was no alternative to travelling on a main road, his bravado matched that of our hosts. Oddly enough, to drive on the left (a traffic pattern that the English share in Europe only with the Swedes) caused him no difficulty—as long as we were in motion. There were occasional tight moments, though, when habit reasserted itself. Leaving a service station in the pretty town of Marlborough, and desiring to turn right, George swung into the near lane—as he would have at home—and found that this manoeuvre had placed us eye to eye with an oncoming double-decker bus. Fortunately it had good brakes, and so did we.

One of the joys of motoring in England is the absence of billboards (the English call them hoardings). We gladly swapped the occasional merriment provoked by Burma Shave signs for the aesthetic satisfaction of gazing at scenes from Constable and Turner. In towns and villages—and we went through one at roughly fifteen-minute intervals—the inn and pub signs were a recurring delight. Sometimes they had been mass-produced by a brewing company, sometimes they had been painted by loving hands at home, and occasionally they were genuine works of art. A pirate with a patch over his eye and pistols crossed over his chest marked The Crossed Arms. A dewy-eyed, fuzzy-maned king of the jungle welcomed us to The White Lion; a big-kneed, green-antlered deer to The White Hart; and a jaunty rooster to The Fighting Cock. George kept hoping we'd see a Cock 'n' Bull, but we never did.

A puzzlement was the occasional sign that labelled a pub as a 'Free House'. 'Maybe they supply free peanuts or potato chips with your second pint of beer,' George guessed.

'Potato *crisps*,' I corrected. 'Potato chips are French fries.'

'I'll bet they're free of some kind of control,' Red said—a guess that was close to the truth. The keepers of free houses have no tie-up with a particular brewer and serve various brands.

At Avebury, George developed the passion for prehistoric stone circles that burned in him undiminished throughout our English year. It was misting that day. Below the dull grey of the sky the trees and grass in the giant Avebury ring had a sombre bronze cast, and the ancient stones dripped water. They're not so very high—three to fifteen feet—but the protective rampart makes up for what they lack in grandeur.

Bounding through long grass, trousers wet to the knees, George explored the ditch that encloses the circle. 'Must be forty feet wide,' he reported in sepulchral tones from below, 'and anyway fifty feet high. Gosh, what an earth-moving job. And without any tools. Isn't that what it says, Red?'

'Not quite,' Red answered, reading the guidebook through a plastic film, then shouting down into the ditch. 'It's supposed to date from the Stone Age; and *they* had tools.'

'I'd sure hate to tackle a job like this with a stone shovel,' George said as he scrambled back to us. 'How big does it say the circle is?'

'Over four hundred yards. It's the largest and the oldest pre-historic monument in Britain.'

'Now, we've *got* to get to Stonehenge.'

We did, some hours later, and it added fuel to the fire. Even in rain—or maybe because of the rain—this much-photographed (and therefore familiar) antiquity was more awesome than I had expected. Unlike Avebury, Stonehenge rises from a flat plain, has no protective nearby village, no encircling embankment. Its huge slabs have the desolate beauty of Ship Rock or other lonely landmarks in the American Southwest, and they seem much higher than their twenty-or-so feet. George was fascinated by the engineering of the lintels that span several of the slabs across the tops—'See how they're morticed!' 'Look at the dovetailing!'— and speculated all the way to Bradford about the method of transport the Bronze Age Britons must have used to haul the 'foreign' stones in Stonehenge all the way from Wales.

Bradford is a charming little town beside the Avon River. (No, not *that* Avon; another one. The name derives from the Celtic word for river, and it pops up all over England on streams miles distant from Stratford.) We paused on the outskirts and got out the yellow book that, together with Ekwall's Dictionary of English Place-Names, the Ogrizek guide to Great Britain, and a sheaf of ordnance maps, formed our motoring library. The yellow book prepared by the Automobile Association, rates hotels by a system of stars, like a Michelin guide, and we were about to stay at a two-star hotel—having been challenged to do so.

It was Roger Mackenzie who had issued the challenge, a twinkle in his eye. 'Five-star hotels are much too grand to be found outside of London,' he had said. 'You might find a four-star hotel in Bath or Bristol, but otherwise I'm afraid you'll have to settle for three stars. A two-star hotel is absolutely unthinkable for Americans, of course, because none of the rooms have private baths. Only the British patronize them. . . .'

So naturally we stayed at a two-star hotel, The Swan, in Bradford. It sold us so thoroughly on two-star hotels that we ever afterward sought them out. But Roger was right about them: we never ran across any other Americans in these citadels of Britishness.

Aside from the fact that our rooms had gables and leaded glass panes in the windows (one of which was stuck shut and one of which was stuck open) and that the view from them down on the High Street of town was delightful, I have forgotten the exact appearance of The Swan in Bradford. I can, however, draw a composite portrait of British two-star hotels:

One enters them through a small dark foyer, in no sense a lobby, and often even bereft of chairs. Its dark wood dado is topped by beige paper patterned in faded scrolls of indeterminate design, much of which is hidden by a notice board on which are posted what the English call adverts for garden fêtes, musicals and other fund-raising events for Disabled Sailors or Distressed Gentlewomen; the monthly programme of the local cinema;

schedules of river trips; and announcements of bargain-priced excursions by coach to Brighton and Woburn Zoo.

Buried deep in a closet-like cubbyhole is a trim little woman in a flowered dress and a crinkly perm. She may, but more often does not, ask the guests with the harsh American accents to register their passport numbers along with their names and addresses, and politely takes no notice of the bemused expression on their faces when she says that the price of their rooms will be twenty-one shillings each. That's approximately three dollars and includes a hearty breakfast. (We could never take this price for granted, and always reacted as if we were getting a rare first edition for twenty-nine cents. The two-star hotel is one of the best buys in Britain—it's a pity they can't export it.)

A porter summoned by a bell that one hears tinkling faintly in the distance pops in, wiping his hands on an apron. Since there are no lifts in two-star hotels, he totes the luggage up the several flights to one's rooms. The staircase, which cants to one side and is carpeted in turkey red, has as many turnings as an English road, plus a tendency to vanish at each floor and start up again around the corner. As one climbs, the porter indicates the location of public rooms—which are on the first floor (the first floor *up*, of course)—and asks if the newcomers would care to stop off in the lounge for tea? No? Then on one forges and is soon in temporary possession of a high-ceilinged room with flowered wallpaper, a washstand, an enormous mahogany wardrobe, one straight chair, and a magnificently comfortable bed with four puffy pillows. Somewhere in the room is the only source of illumination, a forty-watt light bulb, and a gas heater. If fed a shilling, this latter will yield enough warmth to damp-dry socks draped on the rungs of the chair. The bath and the toilet—separate rooms, these—are somewhere down the corridor. They, like the bedrooms, are immaculately clean.

There are no 'Come as You Are' signs outside English hotels, and people *do* dress for dinner—even if 'dressing' consists solely of putting on a fresh blouse. Dinner itself costs approximately a dollar, begins with soup, progresses to lamb with watery Brussels sprouts and two kinds of potatoes, and ends with something custardy. Wholly innocent of seasoning, it's not so much bad as dull. But the linen and glassware are shining bright, the pace is leisurely, the service good, and—New Yorkers, take note—the waitress often smiles.

A sure way to throw an English provincial hotel kitchen staff into an uproar is to ask for coffee with your dinner. The proper time and place are after dinner, in the lounge—a biggish room full of dun-coloured furniture, faded brocade or chintz draperies, gleaming brass bowls full of flowers, and a lithograph of Salisbury Cathedral among the prints on the walls. Here, bathed in the polar glare of blue-white fluorescent lights mounted in the ceiling, one sits and sips in silence, as if performing a sacramental rite—unless the hotel's modernization budget has gone into a television set instead of into fluorescent lights; *then* one sips one's coffee in flickering darkness while Perry Como—yes!—shuffles through a song.

The Swan Hotel in Bradford taught us how to order milk for Red. At breakfast we asked for 'two coffees and one milk.' The milk came in a pitcher, boiling hot, with skin on the top, and Red reacted as if he'd been served hemlock. From then on, whenever we ordered, we were careful to be exact.

'Cold milk, in a glass?' the waitress would quaver. '*Cold* milk, madam?'

'Yes, please. Cold milk, in a glass.' I'd keep my tone carefully matter-of-fact, as if I considered cold milk as sensible a breakfast choice as bloater or pressed ox. The milk was always produced promptly, deliciously fresh, deliciously cool. The English are rather fond of eccentrics, even American ones.

During the night we spent in Bradford, the rain had stopped, and in the morning the town lay spangled in sunshine. We ambled through crooked streets, across a bridge, and into a tiny Saxon church. Of tannish stone, scabrous with age, it was thickset, fortress-like, and sheltering. God must have been much closer to the altar in those early days—before His children learned to elongate arches, fling their churches high, and fill them with light.

There's a tithe barn in Bradford, too, the first we'd seen—or even heard of. We squished down a rutted lane, side-stepped a herd of cows, and eventually found an explanatory plaque. 'Built over a period of 97 years by several Abbesses of Shaftesbury . . . completed in 1350 . . . depot for the collection of that tenth of a man's grain and livestock which he owed to the Abbey,' it said.

The barn was huge, much bigger than the church we'd just left, but it looked more like a modern seed-and-feed storehouse than a fourteenth-century relic. That's because it had a corrugated metal roof and iron scaffolding all along the sides— temporarily, we discovered when we ventured inside. There were half a dozen workmen in the damp gloom, some lost in inky darkness under the roof, some labouring with chisels and buckets of pitch in light admitted through the doorways. A brawny chap, slapping pitch on a hunk of beam that had been laid across sawhorses, stopped whistling 'Some Enchanted Evening' as we took tentative steps across the threshold. He eyed us as we approached, and answered our question before we could frame it. 'Death watch beetle 'as rotted 'er out,' he said. 'From the States, are 'ee?'

On then to Bath, old when the tithe barn at Bradford was new. Julius Caesar didn't sleep there—he never got north of London—but the Emperor Vespasian did; and so did Beau Nash, the dandy who made the town a fashionable eighteenth-century spa. The reason for Bath's long fame is its hot springs, allegedly therapeutic, and certainly relaxing. The magnificent colonnaded Roman bath—which still receives water through the original conduit—caused George to expand his newly born enthusiasm for stone circles to include the engineering know-how of the Romans. I found myself, instead, lost in speculation about the ladies who had ornamented those tiled decks and pillared corridors some 1,700 years ago; bits of delicately crafted gold jewellery, exquisite tortoise-shell combs, and smooth-polished ointment jars remain to indicate that they were women of taste. Red's interest was concentrated on a series of stone markers that the occupation forces had set up along the roads of Britain and that have now been gathered into the museum at Bath. 'To the Lady Nemesis most sacred, Vettius Benignus pays his vow,' one said. It's a thrill for a Latin scholar, especially a fledgling, to decipher even a single word from an original source.

But there's more to Bath than baths. Overlooking the Roman relics is a sixteenth-century lace-paper valentine, Bath Abbey. This light and airy Gothic cathedral is not the first church to rest on this site, but the only trace of earlier structures lies in a list on one wall of the present cathedral.

'Look, Red,' I said, 'here's what I meant about living history.'

See how the list begins with an abbess named Bernguidis, in 681?
And how the last Saxon name was Wulfwold, in 1061?'
  'Battle-of-Hastings-1066,' Red intoned, reciting a date that
every schoolboy memorizes. 'Sure. The title changes to "Prior"
right afterwards. Look; there's a French name, Walter de Anno,
in 1261.'
  My eye continued down the list. 'You can see surnames
evolving too,' I said. 'Hugh or John was enough, at first. But
by the sixteenth century, the heads of church had modern names
like William Holeway, there. I wonder why they changed the
title to Rector?'
  'I don't think that surname theory of yours is right, Mom,' my
son objected. 'The single names could have belonged to monks
and the rectors could have been ordinary clergymen. The timing
is just right, because Henry VIII dissolved all the monasteries
sometime in the 1500s.'
  Bath was our first English cathedral, and we tiptoed through
it very respectfully. In most American churches one doesn't feel
the presence of people unless they are actually there beside you,
but even when empty an English church throbs with life. That's
because it's a sort of family Bible for its parish or see, its walls
being studded with memorial plaques or lined with tombs of
long-gone V.I.P.s, and the tattered banners of some ancient,
valiant regiment may hang from its vaulted archways or pillars.
All of which give it an air both solemn and stately. Hence it was
a shock and a delight to see, in Bath Abbey, a slotted black box
with a sign on it that said: 'Archdeacon's Box. Questions,
Suggestions, Objections, Help for Lame Dogs, Anything.'
  We never saw a wisecrack like this in any other English
church; it may have reflected the sophisticated and cosmopolitan
character of this particular town. Even if the Romans had never
laid an inch of pipe there, Bath would be worth visiting for its
magnificent Georgian houses and the Circus and Crescents
around which they curve. The guidebook said, and accurately,
'So cleverly has Bath preserved its sense of the past that you
expect at any moment to encounter fat, smiling Pickwick.'
Which is quite a feat, in as much as modern motor traffic is about
as thick as in Oxford, and TV aerials sprout from the roof tops
like lightning rods in Kansas.
  Like Rome, Bath is a city poised on seven hills, and there are

more of the same to the south of it. The country is rocky and bleak, with starved-looking farms clinging to the hillsides, limestone quarries in abundance, and subterranean rivers flowing through caves under one's feet. We had intended to pause briefly in the city of Wells and drive then to Glastonbury, which legend says was the site of Camelot. But we didn't, partly because the drizzle that had come on at noon was a driving rain by the time we got to Wells, and partly because even in driving rain Wells Cathedral is so impressive one simply *can't* pause briefly.

We found rooms at The Swan—two out of three English two-star hotels are called The Swan—and then stood at our windows staring in awe and admiration at the pile of rain-black stone across the way. It is smaller than Bath Abbey, older and less lacy, and, we thought, more beautiful. Facing us were two square towers, between which sculptured figures in arched niches rose in vertical columns across the entire façade. The sky was beginning to clear, and against a patch of clear blue in the east a central, higher tower was silhouetted, this one with delicate pinnacles probing the sky. The over-all effect was of great dignity and strength.

'It's getting pretty dark,' George said, 'but would you like to go over there anyway?'

We would, and in twilight hush we made our first acquaintance with one of the great treasures of Britain. The nave is framed by thick pillars, each a cluster of smaller columns, that are briefly interrupted by ornamental capitals before they soar into Gothic arches. The famous arches of Wells, however, are the inverted ones in the centre of the cathedral. Joined point to point with upstanding arches on the four sides where the transepts cross the nave, like hourglasses, they not only support the weight of the central tower but also add architectural dynamism to the interior. Pointed arches carry the eye up but do not bring it down. Not so at Wells: there is a stirring sense of motion in these arches, a majestic rise and fall and rise again, the rhythm of waves at sea.

On this particular late afternoon the ceiling had vanished in brooding obscurity, shadows were deepening within the cathedral itself, and our footfalls echoed hollowly as we moved swiftly along. Then we came upon the Chapter House stair. I could wish nothing better for other tourists than that they should approach it as we did, out of a vast and gloomy church, and find it suffused by cold light filtered through rain clouds. The staircase is narrow, edged by clustered columns and arched openings, and appears even higher than it is because of the sharply vaulted ceiling overhead. The stone treads, hollowed by the passage of countless feet, curve, halfway up, toward a doorway on the right. The light lay luminously along the irregular hollows in the steps at the base of the staircase, then fell fully on the risers of the steps above us, and because a greater area was illuminated as one's glance was pulled upward, the light seemed to grow brighter. It gathered itself, finally, into a wedge of whiteness at the point where the stairs vanished. The scene had the emotional impact of a white wax taper burning in the dark. It was tantalizing, too. What mystery lay beyond? Heaven itself?

What *did* lie beyond was a lovely room, circular and delicately fan-vaulted, with stone niches where cathedral officials sit for chapter meetings. But it was no more than lovely, and even the staircase had lost its ethereal splendour by the next morning, when we raced back to take a photograph of it. By then creamy sunlight was pouring down the steps, suffusing stairs and walls alike with cheerful radiance. It was beautiful still, but in flat light it was stripped of mystery. One knew that the curving steps would lead to a man-made room.

The whole cathedral was different in the morning. Warm and human. A gnarled old man was vacuuming the rug in front of the lectern. The church ladies were twittering away as they arranged their bouquets. Somewhere off-stage we heard the starts and stops of a choir rehearsal, and in due course the choirmaster led his boys—the littlest one skipping in order to keep up—into the stalls. A blue velour rope was drawn across the transepts to keep the curious out, but those sweet, clear voices formed a background, like the murmur of a brook, to our further explorations in adjacent aisles.

There was humour in the cathedral, too. Wells has a famous fourteenth-century astronomical clock, out of which, when the hour strikes, knights come galloping. In opposite circles, round and round they go, lances poised, each giving the other an awful wallop as they pass. There's another kind of animated clock on the north side of the cathedral; and a series of small sculptures in the nave that *almost* move, so vigorous and free is the carving.

These are tucked into the curlicues of the capitals on the pillars, and are a lively record of thirteenth-century rural England.

Interested in fashion, whatever the century, I noted the men's Dutch bobs, their helmets and cowls, their leggings and boots. George, the farm boy ascendant, prowled under the figures of countrymen, muttering, 'Pitchforks with only *two* tines?' Red found a series of figures that told a story: of thieves who had stolen apples, or maybe potatoes; were caught; and beaten. Their rigid fingers spoke eloquently of pain. There were birds and flowers and reptiles, and all manner of living creatures memorialized in stone, and the six hundred years between them and us quite melted away.

While George and Red, having paid a shilling for the privilege, climbed to the top of the central tower, I made a pilgrimage from tomb to tomb, standing over the effigies of bishops long since turned to dust, studying their carefully arranged garments; expressionless faces, and unseeing eyes, trying to imagine what they were like in life. If I had been living here in the fourteenth or fifteenth century, would one of them have baptized Red at the cathedral's Norman font? Or would they have been too grand for that rite? Come to think of it, what status in life would *I* have had?

When the men returned, they reported their finds, seen from on high: a moat on the south, and a 'pretty little row of houses on a dead-end street to the north.' The proper name for this latter is a close, and the one at Wells was built in the fourteenth century. It was a fit subject for a Come-to-Britain ad. It enclosed a chain of identical small stone houses with identical chimney stacks, like toy soldiers lined up on a nursery floor, that stood shoulder to shoulder behind their common low stone wall, geraniums and dahlias making tidy splashes of colour in their identical dooryards.

The moat, on the other side of the cathedral, encircled the Bishop's Palace. This, a series of buildings facing into a quadrangle like an Oxford college, was of the same stone and of the same period as the cathedral and had the same feeling of dignity and strength. We joined a little knot of sight-seers at the edge of the drawbridge, to watch the performing swans. Twice a day they sail up to a bellpull dangling from a window on the moat and give it a tug. An anonymous hand then tosses out bread.

There are ducks in the moat, too—beautiful irridescent mallards among them—and what entranced us most about the feeding ceremony was to see how the ducks held back, in an outer ring, until the regal swans had fed. 'And that,' said George in his professor-of-biology voice, 'is what is meant by pecking order.'

Having dallied so joyously in this exquisite cathedral town, there was no time left for Glastonbury, or the Cheddar Gorge, or Exeter, or much of anything else. Red's school took up in two days, and the name tags had yet to be sewn on his clothes, so we lit out for Oxford.

I have reflected often, since, upon our good fortune in having gone exactly where we did that first time out. A question often asked us in later months was, 'Are you getting to see anything of the *real* England?' and our questioner always relaxed and smiled with approval when I catalogued the sights we had seen on that first trip. Part of our joy in it, of course, could have been due to novelty and our own romantic expectations. There was a honeymoon haze over everything during those first few weeks. But the lingering enchantment of that trip was due in greater part to the fact that what we saw was choice. Stonehenge, Bath, and the cathedral city of Wells are all best-of-show. Our later wanderings demonstrated that in no other direction from Oxford are there so many miles of consistently lovely countryside, and never again in one journey did we stumble upon such a richly complementary series of ancient buildings and towns.

Occasionally now I swap experiences with other Americans who have visited England, most of them having 'done' it in a week or less as a fragment of a European tour. Shortness of time and the fixed ideas of travel agents or hotel porters have usually led them to equate rural England with the bus run between London and Stratford, and the best that many of them have to say about the trip is, 'It was awfully pretty in stretches.' So is the drive from New York to Boston, but it is not my idea of the *real* America. What we experienced on that first outing in England was comparable to a journey across upper New York State at its brilliant best, or a circle tour from Monterey to San Francisco to Carmel on our own West Coast.

Chapter 4

AT THE END of Red's first day at school he let himself in so quietly I didn't hear him. But when the hall door creaked, I pounced. 'Well, how did it go?'

'All right.'

'I mean, *really*. Tell me about it.'

'It was O.K.'

'Were the boys friendly?'

'They were O.K.'

'Meet anyone you especially liked?'

'Mom! On the first day?'

Then I noticed—much too belatedly—that Red was wearing his shuttered look. He gets it whenever his aunts tell him how much he's grown since his last birthday or whenever family visitors impale him with a 'Well, Son, and what are your ambitions in life?' So I shut up. I don't know yet whether his first day at school was an utterly bewildering and painful experience or only mildly unsettling.

However, within two weeks such phrases as 'jolly good' began to pepper his speech, homework had changed to 'prep', and anything that was both trivial and useless had become a 'waffle'. His accent on words like 'necessary' began to shift forward, and before long he (alone in the family) was unselfconsciously saying 'lehzure' and 'shedule'.

He began to come home brimful of classroom anecdotes about Sid and Froggy, who turned out to be not schoolmates but masters. They were nicknamed so irreverently as a reaction, I dare say, to the formal 'sir', which had to be incorporated in speaking to them at school. One of his earliest, and most pleasant, discoveries was that they were human, in the mass neither better nor worse than the teachers he had had in Pasadena. (Incidentally, there is no more acute judge of a teacher's ability than a teen-age schoolboy.) 'The only way they differ from the ones I've had at home,' he said, 'is that it's harder here for the class to get 'em off the subject of the lesson and on to personal reminiscences.'

In his early weeks he had both a minor triumph in class and what seemed at the time to be a major disaster. The triumph came about this way:

'We've been reviewing Latin grammar, you know, and today we got into the negative imperative. I knew the sentence on the blackboard, but the other boys didn't have a clue.'

I interrupted. 'Hah! And American school children are supposed to be so far behind the English!'

'Hey, let me finish. Ben—that's Mr Thomson—tried to drag the answer out of the class, and couldn't, and finally he said, "Well, I suppose it's understandable. You had this verb form such a long time ago." The reason I knew it, Mom, was because I learned it *just before I left home.*'

The disaster involved a theme, for the writing of which class time was allowed. Accustomed to the assignment of such essay titles as 'My Summer Vacation' or 'Why I Liked This Book', the title assigned for *this* essay threw Red into a flat spin. It was 'The Joys of Poverty'. He used up most of his time trying to decide what joys there might *be* in poverty (never, as a child of this affluent generation, having known any), wrote a sentence or two in his workbook, and decided that he'd polish it at home that evening. But, no; this essay was to have been completed during the class period. The workbooks were collected, and when they were returned. Red found himself looking at the only failing grade I believe he's ever received. It was a nasty shock, but a salutary one, and—I'm jumping ahead, now—by year's end, he had learned to organize his thoughts so well and express himself so clearly that his composition was better than that of many college students in the United States.

There were a number of American boys at the school. Some of them committed a breach of etiquette at the school's first Rugby (pronounced 'Rugger') match. Watching the St. Edward's five scoop up the ball after a stupid fumble by the M.C.S. team, several of the Americans had booed. Red had not been at the game, but he *was* at the school assembly when the Master cut the booers down to size. 'He shredded 'em into little pieces,' Red reported, adding, with awe, 'And he never even raised his voice.'

Fresh from the land of sis-boom-bah and kill-the-ump, the

Americans had a hard time at first learning to applaud good
play by *either* team. They were allowed to yell, 'Good show!'
or 'School! School!' although Red says that I am wrong to add
those exclamation marks, that they suggest too much unbridled
emotion. But in time the image of cheerleaders and baton
twirlers faded from the young American minds, and they learned
(to their everlasting benefit) the basic lesson of British sportsman-
ship—that it isn't who wins but how the game is played that
counts.

Rugby is a fast, hard-driving game similar to football; but is
played without helmets, shoulder pads, or other protective
devices. Our only other information about the game came from
the salesman who sold Red his Rugby boots.

'Ever played Rugger, lad?' he had asked.

'No, I haven't,' Red had replied, his gaze riveted on the
wicked-looking cleats studding the boot soles.

The salesman had said, handing over the boots, 'Boy, it's
murder!'

Not surprisingly, therefore, Red approached his first match
with something less than galloping enthusiasm. He came drag-
ging home with mud in his hair and mud *inside* his shorts; he
looked, in fact, as if he'd been wallowing in the field instead of
running across it. He also had a cut on his hand. I got all fluttery
and maternal.

'Cut it out, Mom,' he said, parrying my attempts to bandage
his hand. 'The ground was slippery because it was misting, and
I kept falling down. That's why I'm so muddy. Nobody pushed
me. The game actually isn't as rough as I expected. In fact,
whenever it *did* get rough, one of the fellows would sing out,
"What do you think this is—Yank football?"'

One of the best things about the school was that the boys
accepted him as an individual, and not as an oddity by reason
of his nationality. Oh, once in a while someone would try to
imitate his American accent in order to ridicule it, but Red
could never accept this as a personal insult, since it sounded so
funny to him too. 'Like trying to talk hillbilly with a clothespin
on your nose,' was how he described it. 'You just ought to *hear*
how they say, "Reach for the sky, podnuh!"' Forewarned, he
had let his crew-cut grow out before we arrived in England, and
the only real ragging he got was directed at his 'Teddy boy shoes'.

They looked bizarre to his schoolmates, because of the moccasin welt.

I was collecting a host of questions about the school. What were the 'sets' he occasionally mentioned? His 'house'? What was the rôle of the 'prefects'? The sixth form included the oldest boys, and it differed in some way from the others, but how? I decided that the answers could wait, though, until I'd solved some of my domestic problems. I couldn't seem to get *settled*. But my mind was easier, now that I knew Red was making friends and the strain of being a stranger was wearing off.

I quit worrying about him altogether the day he said, 'Birkett and I tried lunch at the Muni'—the Municipal Restaurant, a cafeteria not far from the school—'and it wasn't bad. Only a shilling, too.'

'Only a shilling. *Fourteen cents?* At that price, what on earth did they give you?'

'The daily special. I don't know what was in it.'

'A meat dish?'

'I guess so. With potatoes and bread and Jell-O.'

'Well, what did the meat look like? What shape was it?'

'Lumps.'

'What colour was it?'

'Sort of grey.'

'What texture?'

'Soft.'

'Good grief, Red!'

'But it was nice and hot, Mom.'

Any intelligent workingwoman who is also a housewife and mother learns to streamline and organize her household routine. For years I'd done my marketing and household chores on a once-a-week basis, and then on a big scale. I am also a great one for storing kitchen utensils and house-cleaning equipment at the site of use, and for arranging furniture and household accessories so that nothing has to be stepped over, walked around, edged past, moved closer, or pushed out of the way. These habits died hard. The keeping limit of our 'fridge' was three days, and I couldn't carry home enough food to last us a week, anyway—even after I acquired a wicker shopping cart. I made good progress in routinizing the household chores, although George did boggle occasionally at my idea of breakfast priorities: first the Rayburn got fed, and then the family. But I never succeeded in rearranging the furniture so that any of us could ignore it.

It was my search for an extension cord—I wanted to position a lamp close enough to a chair so the occupant wouldn't have to sit sidesaddle when he read—that acquainted us with an idiosyncrasy of English houses that has been far less publicized than their plumbing or heating but it is of the same order. English electric outlets are simple enough in themselves, but to get any juice out of them requires an awesome superstructure of custom-fitted plugs and adaptors and causes the baseboards of English rooms to bristle like hedgehogs. Here's why:

1—Electrical outlets are designed to supply a specific amount of amperage. These outlets are called points, although they don't have any, being punctured instead by three holes.

2—These holes are spaced differently in outlets of differing amperage. For example, the holes are bigger and farther apart in a 15-amp. outlet than in a 5-amp. outlet.

3—Since appliances are designed to require a certain amount of amperage, their plugs have three prongs sized and spaced to fit the outlet whose amperage delivery corresponds to the amperage requirement of the appliance.

Pretty neat scheme, eh? It protects heedless or stupid citizens from the consequences of plugging an appliance requiring fifteen amperes into an outlet that can deliver only five.

But there's a hitch.

What if a room contains only a 15-amp. outlet, and the householder wishes to plug into it a heater that requires 5 amps? He's out of luck, because 5-amp. prongs aren't spaced to fit 15-amp. holes. Suppose, too, that he has a 2-amp. lamp. *Its* prongs won't fit 15-amp. holes either. One solution would be to put 15-amp. plugs on both appliances, but then of course they could be plugged in only one at a time. And think of the waste, using only 5 amps. or 2 amps. when all those *other* amps. are available but untapped.

Therefore, the adaptor was invented.

This gadget comes in varying amperages too. It has prongs that fit the holes in a given-size outlet, but its surface is studded with holes, properly spaced for plugs of lower amperages. The combinations and permutations of holes in adaptors are astronomical. The first time I examined the display of adaptors at Shergold's the Headington ironmonger, the bounty dazzled me. Three conferences with one husband and two ironmongers later, I discovered that one can indeed find an adaptor for any combination of appliances except a 5-amp. adaptor into which can be plugged two 2-amp. appliances, which was the kind we needed. With such adaptors in one's outlets one can then plug in appliances almost as freely as in an American house—unless, of course, the outlets in a given room won't carry the amperage of a particular appliance. In that case one either rewires the house or uses a broom instead of a vacuum cleaner. A broom gets into the corners better, anyway. Our particular choice was whether to sit in the dining-room, which was warm because it had the only 15-amp. outlet in the house and therefore was the site of a high-wattage electric heater, or to sit in the living-room, which had comfortable chairs but was cold because it had only a 5-amp. outlet.

I shall mention for the record but with elaboration the fact that some appliances have plugs with two prongs instead of three. Some plugs come with built-in fuses and require special kinds of adaptors. Equally specialized converters and adaptors are necessary if one wishes to plug 110-volt American appliances into 230-volt English outlets. (We decided not to mix our volts. We had our hands full dealing with the English ones.) We were also spared the necessity of coping with square-prong plugs for square-hole outlets—a new type of installation that was just beginning to catch on. At one of our conferences with the ironmonger Mr Shergold told George that great efforts are being made in England to establish the new square-prong plugs and square-hole outlets as standard. George said, dead-pan, that he thought such standardization would be a good idea.

Oh yes. I never got an extension cord.

I had spotted, with delight, a launderette within easy walking distance, and assumed that I could use it as I do the one I patronize at home—for the rough-dry laundering of such items as towels, bed linen, and cotton knit underwear. But, alas, it had no dryers. For an extra penny one could whirl one's wetwash around in a drum called an extractor, and then tote it home to dry on clotheslines in the garden.

I tried this for a while, but it wasn't satisfactory. The laundry didn't dry on wet days because I was usually somewhere else when the showers began, and by the time I got home the terry towels were dripping their sodden selvages into the Brussels sprouts. And the laundry didn't dry on dry days, either, unless there was a good brisk wind. It took me two weeks before I suddenly realized why there was no warmth to the sun: it was never overhead, but spun around the garden at tree-top level. When I shared this exciting intelligence with the family at dinner, Red gave me a compassionate glance, and said, 'My gosh, Mom, we're fifty-two degrees north. What else did you expect?' Foreign residence has great value, I've decided, for women who don't understand what fifty-two degrees north means until they wonder why there's never any hot sun on their clotheslines.

Eventually I gave up, bought a rack and installed it in the solarium. We came, in time, to accept as normal the sight of wet underpants banked by ferns.

That was after Lady Headington had left town, however. I didn't make any radical changes while she was still dropping in to collect her mail—and, incidently, to check up on my housekeeping habits. I soon learned that one doesn't have to offer tea. Instant coffee will do very well, and the two of us had many a chummy cup together at England's coffee-break hour, 11 a.m.

One morning when she arrived I was putting away my groceries. Included in the lot was a box of eggs, and as I tucked them into the fridge, Lady Headington suddenly asked, 'Why don't Americans eat boiled eggs?'

'They don't?' I said, startled. 'How queer.' Then, realizing that she was talking about us, I asked, 'What makes you think so?'

'A friend of mine who visited one of your large cities—Boston, I believe—told me there weren't any eggcups on sale in the shops.'

I suppressed a smile. 'Perhaps she didn't look in the right departments,' I said. 'One can buy eggcups in the United States, and people do eat boiled eggs. But my way of serving them is to remove them from the shell and transfer them to custard cups.'

From the bemused expression that spread over her face it was obvious that eating boiled eggs from custard cups is just as peculiar as not eating them at all.

Lady Headington was a widow, I learned, who lived in Oxford because she had long loved its beauty and the tone given it by the university. But we should have come before the war, she said, before what she obliquely referred to as 'the present situation' had developed. The twin causes of her disaffection, I discovered, were the welfare state and the Morris Motor Works (both of which seem clearly destined to endure).

The heavy truck traffic on the street outside caused everything loose in the house to vibrate, and one day as she listened to the ship's clock stutter when it struck, she said, 'This was always such a lovely, quiet street, before there were so many factories at Cowley. Lord Nuffield has been a great benefactor to the university, I can't deny that, but I do wish he had started repairing his bicycles somewhere else.'

Nevertheless, the workman who was then William Morris *did* expand his bicycle repair shop and garage on Oxford's Holywell Street into the gigantic empire that now produces England's best-selling motor-car. The Morris Works, along with a complex of steel fabricators and other heavy industry, has dug itself into a big wedge of countryside that lies south-east of Oxford, and with its growth has changed Oxford from a sleepy university town into a booming industrial city. There is good reason now for wags to call the university 'the Latin Quarter of Oxford', and it is accurate enough that the only civic greeting posted at the railroad station is a large sign that says, 'Welcome to Oxford, Home of Pressed Steel'. As an economic entity the town could function perfectly well if the university and the colleges vanished overnight.

Lady Headington didn't like the class of people who had been attracted to Oxford by ready jobs in the factories. She warned us to beware of the rough crowd who frequented the pub across the street, and urged us to call the police if the noise got out of hand. 'They aren't people from this neighbourhood,' she said. 'They come over here from one of the council housing estates near Marston.' She spoke with the same distaste one sometimes hears in America when 'those people who live in the slum clearance projects' are mentioned.

(Actually, we found that the people who frequented the pub were well behaved and orderly, and after they observed how much trouble George had in garaging our car when their cars were parked bumper to bumper at the opposite curb, they tried to leave turning space for him.)

Lady Headington had paid a colossal sum to have the house

redecorated, and her most frequent lament was that in England today one can't get any service from people in the service trades. She was dead right on *that* one; higher paid jobs in the Morris Works certainly created an acute shortage of domestic workers and repairmen in Oxford. Among the businessmen screaming for help was the present proprietor of the Morris Garage on Holywell Street, who advertised week after week, in increasingly urgent terms, for a repairman. There was a sins-of-the-father quality about this situation that I found singularly affecting.

Nor did Lady Headington like the 'new' university—no longer the exclusive preserve of the rich and the well born, but now an institution to which admission is gained primarily on the basis of academic ability. When family position and financial resources determined who went to university in England, many a young man grew grey at Oxford. But now that three out of four undergraduates, having passed competitive exams to qualify for entrance, are financed by the government, the male equivalent of America's college widow is in residence no longer. A certain zaniness and charm of manner have vanished with him; things just aren't done as *nicely* any more.

'I can remember the time when a few undergraduates might have brought shopgirls to the spring boat races on the river,' Lady Headington remarked, 'but they most certainly never married them. Now, I dare say'—her mouth drawing into a thin line—'some are comfortable *only* with shopgirls.'

Thus, she introduced us to a theme that was often to recur in conversation with upper-class English conservatives: nostalgia for the good old days before the welfare state had corrupted the working classes.

I crowned the morning coffee breaks by inviting Lady Headington to dinner, at which I gave her a typical Sunday-on-the-farm menu: fried chicken, mashed potatoes with gravy, and chocolate cake à la mode. She was polite about it, if not really rapturous, and especially praised the cake. I thought it a bit of all right, myself, because I'd baked it in the Rayburn. The icing hid the cracks.

Two days later, convinced at last that we were not wild Indians (red), she went off to Africa to visit relatives. Our correspondence thereafter took on a ritualistic pattern. My letters began, 'I'm sorry to have to report that the refrigerator has ceased functioning altogether this time'—or that a paraffin heater had smoked up the living-room wallpaper, or that the roof had leaked, or that a bit of wall had collapsed. Her replies began, 'I am sorry that you are having trouble with the refrigerator' or whatever it was— 'and would suggest that you take it up *directly* with Cooper's. They assured me . . .'

We had a living link with Lady Headington, however, in the person of Mrs Iris Blount, her—and our—'daily'. Domestic workers aren't called 'chars' any more, at least in Oxford. They're too scarce. Another few years of famine and they will be, as in America, 'the lady who comes in to help'. Characteristically, they work only a few hours a week, for spending money. And they are not disposed to slave for anybody. As long as England is prosperous, Mrs Blount and her kind will dwindle in numbers, as they have in the United States, and the English housewife who used to have servants will do without them.

I could have done without Mrs Blount, because all she did in the four hours a week she allotted to us was to lay a fresh coat of wax over last week's coat of wax in bathroom and kitchen. But I would have missed one of the greatest delights of the Oxford year if she hadn't come on Tuesdays and Fridays to share her wit and wisdom with me.

She was a wiry little woman with straight brown hair, sharp features, raw, roughened hands, and a complexion that always reflected in its colour the vagaries of the weather. She came whizzing up to the house on a bicycle in whose basket she carried the fleece-lined house slippers in which she liked to work. Her first move after getting into these slippers was to run around the house opening all the windows and doors in order to admit some good English air into a house that I persisted in keeping stuffily hot. I then closed the doors and windows unobtrusively as possible, and she reopened them as unobtrusively as possible, neither one of us taking official notice of the other's action.

Mrs Blount was a kitchen philospher. She would suddenly pause in the midst of her waxing and say, 'Mrs Beadle.'

I'd respond, 'Yes?'

'I always say you get out of folks just what you put into them.'

'I say the same, Mrs Blount.'

Then she'd resume her waxing.

Or: 'There's talk at the Works'—her husband was employed at

the Morris plant—'of a strike. Now, if you please, what's the sense of another strike? A man gets a raise and up go his wife's prices. But'—slap! slap! with the waxing cloth—'does he give her any more money? No! The wives ought to strike for stabilized prices. That's what *I* say.'

Mrs Blount was a local woman, although her speech was not as thickly overlaid with Oxfordshire dialect as that of the gardener, who dropped his h's like 'ailstones. There was nothing wrong with her brain: she got the American monetary system straight after one telling, whereas I never understood the British system; and she was at least no more confused that I was about the difference between Republicans and Democrats. But she was naïve about a great many things. She believed the weather predictions in the almanac, for example, her faith in no way dimmed by the fact that the predictions were invariably wrong, and the amount of medical misinformation she possessed—and acted upon—was encyclopaedic. The highlight of an outing to London with some ladies of the Mothers' Union was having her shoes blacked. 'It was in Charing Cross I had it done,' she said. 'I've never seen a bootblack before. I thought they just had them in America.'

I thoroughly enjoyed her company. She enjoyed mine. I expect both of us, on Tuesdays and Fridays, regaled our families with anecdotes about the other's odd ways. But our mutual affection was based on more than the entertainment value to be derived from our differing backgrounds and the differing cultures that had produced us. I admired her for her forthright honesty and good humour. She felt protective toward us, strangers in her land.

One day when I was out she reported that a phone call had come in for George. The caller had been a man 'with a funny way of speaking—a foreigner, I dare say.' Their conversation had gone like this:

'Have I the home of Professor Beadle?'

'Yes.'

'Is the Professor there?'

'No.'

'Can you tell me what time he will return?'

'No.'

'Well'—the caller was evidently striving for a light touch—'at least, I have located his home, have I not?'

At this point in her recital Mrs Blount turned a worried face to me. 'Mrs Beadle, that's what gangsters do, you know.'

'Oh, Mrs Blount,' I replied. 'You've been seeing too many American movies on television.'

'No,' she insisted, 'that's how it is. A gangster finds out where somewhere lives, and the next thing the whole family is dead in their beds.'

'So then what did you say to the man on the telephone?' I prompted.

'I hung up,' she said.

Chapter 5

ONE FINE DAY in October, Cyril Darlington—Oxford's professor of botany, a tall, handsome man with the bearing of a Roman senator—said to George, 'Convocation is meeting in an hour. Why don't you come along with me?'

'I can't,' George replied, having been cramming a bit on university protocol. 'I don't have a gown, And if I had, I couldn't wear it. I don't have a degree yet.'

He has seven, in fact. What he meant was that he didn't have an *Oxford* degree. The university forbids the wearing of academic regalia other than its own, and in order to get visiting professors like George into acceptable garb it routinely awards them an Oxford M.A. degree.

'Borrow a gown and come along anyway,' the Prof said. 'It'll be all right.'

'Tell you what,' my husband rejoined. 'I'll run over to College and ask the secretary about it. I might as well find out when I'm supposed to get that degree.'

The secretary told him, 'I think you already *have* a degree. Wasn't it granted by decree?'

'Nobody told me,' he replied.

So the secretary called the registry. Yes, Professor Beadle did have an M.A. degree. 'Then,' asked the secretary, 'may he attend Convocation today?'

'No, I'm sorry,' said the registry. 'He hasn't signed a matriculation form.'

George hurried over and signed the form, borrowed a gown, hood, and mortarboard from the college porter, and set off with a Botany Department demonstrator (the equivalent of an assistant professor) to Convocation.

'You're not wearing a white bow tie,' his companion told him. 'So you mustn't wear your hood. A hood can be worn only with a white tie.'

George stuffed the hood in his pocket.

At the Sheldonian Theatre they found Prof Darlington, who

remarked to my husband, 'Too bad you don't have a hood.'

'I have. It's in my pocket. I can't wear it because I don't have a white tie.'

'Oh, that rule doesn't apply to this particular Convocation.'

So George put on his hood.

Convocation was impressive, he told me. But he didn't pay as much attention as he should have to the business of the day—partly because a lot of it was translated in Latin, and partly because he was too occupied counting white-ties-with-hoods, coloured-ties-with-hoods, and coloured-ties-without-hoods. The three categories, as far as he could tell, were neck and neck.

A few days later I happened to be in the vicinity of the Sheldonian as another university ceremony was about to begin. The Sheldonian, by the way, is just up the street from Balliol, on The Broad. As one rounds the corner from Cornmarket Street, one's gaze is pulled along a concave line of buildings directly to this seventeenth-century neoclassic masterpiece of Christopher Wren, its roof surmounted by a gallery and a gleaming white cupola. Interspersed in the railings of the fence that surrounds the circular grey stone building are pedestals on which perch the leprous, weather-beaten busts of—maybe—Roman Emperors. Max Beerbohm thought they were, anyway, and it was on their brows that great beads of perspiration glistened when Beerbohm's Edwardian enchantress, Zuleika Dobson, glided past the Sheldonian in her landau that May Monday in 1910 or so.

The young women whom I saw gathering on that same spot were not of Zuleika's ilk. Nice-enough girls, clean-scrubbed and tidy, but unlikely to inspire mass drownings because of unrequited love. They looked a bit like magpies, in their limp black academic caps, black academic gowns, white shirts with black string ties, black skirts, black stockings, and black shoes. There were clusters of men in The Broad, too, in similar dark garb, except that their heads were covered with square mortarboards, and white bow ties glistened under their chins.

I knew why they had gathered. Term had begun, and these new undergraduates were going in coveys to the Sheldonian for the matriculation ceremony, which would make them, officially, members of the university. I also knew—I'd been doing some cramming too—that for them to be members of this university was quite unlike being students at Harvard or the University of Michigan or Caltech, or any other American university.

One of Oxford's favourite jokes—in which the protagonist is usually American—has to do with the tourist who asks a native to direct him to the university. A variant has a dumb bloke from Kansas searching for 'the campus'. Neither, of course, can be found. The university is a human institution and a way of life, not a physical entity. It welcomes the scholars, establishes the broad outlines of their courses, provides lectures for them, examines them, and grants their degrees, And for this it needs a few buildings. Among them are the Sheldonian Theatre, which I was then facing, the Bodleian Library just behind it, the Examination Schools on High Street, and the science labs on South Parks Road—where, presumably, George was at that moment deep in the business of making notes for his first lecture series.

But such campuses as will be found at Oxford—in the American sense of a grouping of buildings on common acreage—are those that exist within the walled and cloistered colleges, some thirty in number. Balliol's layout was typical, although by now I knew that its buildings and gardens were not particularly distinguished. (As soon as I had convinced myself that the Rayburn was not going to blow up in my absence, I had launched a regular programme of visitation, and by early October had ticked off a round dozen colleges.) The older colleges are clustered in the centre of the town, some with common walls, others separated by the markets and shops, garages and hotels of the city. Most of the women's colleges and that other nineteenth-century addition, Keble College, are on the fringes of the city centre, to the north. It is fashionable in Oxford to look down one's nose at Keble, a mammoth jukebox of multicoloured brick in a style of architecture described by its detractors as 'Early Bloody'. The newest college, just-finished Nuffield (gift of the head of the Morris Works and bearing his name) is hard by the railroad station, on the west. Nuffield is also the butt of gibes—for its 'brazen spire atop a Cotswold cottage'. But I rather liked the Victorian lustiness of Keble, and I suspect that the main strike against Nuffield is that it's new. Give it twenty years of smoke from the trains across the way, and it ought to have an acceptable Oxford patina.

The Oxford colleges got their start in the Middle Ages. They were simple rooming houses at first, with a master in charge to see that the young scholars behaved themselves and got enough to eat. From these halls they went out to lectures given under the auspices of the university. If a boy had a bit of trouble with his Latin, nothing could have been more natural than to ask help from the house master; and so a teaching function was added to the colleges. They are still the basic social and instructional units at Oxford.

Modern undergraduates come to the university ready to concentrate in one narrow field of scholarship. The liberal-arts bias that encourages American college students to sample widely of varied course offerings does not exist at Oxford; the programme there is more similar to that of the graduate schools at American universities. Oxford has fourteen areas of speciality, of which the most demanding and the most honoured is Ancient Philosophy and History, a course known simply as 'Greats'.

Whereas the American student 'majors' in a subject, the Oxford undergraduate 'reads' it. Literally. His work is directed from his college by one or two tutors who are experts in his chosen field. For three or four years, in a weekly private session, he presents an essay based on his reading, hears his mentor discuss and criticize it, may be forced to defend it, is finally sent on his way with a new reading assignment and a new essay topic. That's all there is to the academic side of an Oxford education: Mark Hopkins on one end of a log and a student on the other. It's the best possible method of teaching, and also the most expensive. The cost can be justified only if teacher and pupil are of top intellectual calibre.

Given close fellowship with brilliant minds in an elegant and civilized setting, it is not surprising that the Oxonian's loyalty and affection go first to the company of people with whom he has lived. (That's all that 'collegium' means, anyway— a company of like-minded people.) The American university graduate identifies himself as a Yale man, but the graduate of Oxford is likely to tell you that he was at Balliol.

It has been this way almost from the beginning. Nobody remembered the university with special affection. It was only cold lecture halls and colder-eyed examiners. Therefore, the rents from a bit of property or some fine silver plate passed from a fond graduate to Merton or Exeter or Queen's, or to whatever college was his ancient English equivalent of good old Kappa Sig. Hence, over the years, the colleges grew wealthy, developed into wholly autonomous institutions, became more important and more powerful than the university. Although they have now been forced to yield ground to the university for the maintenance of the modern science labs that no individual college can afford, they are still far more than the administrative subdivisions that the word 'college' connotes to Americans when it occurs within the context of university organization here.

Just how important the colleges are George had discovered when he'd gone to the Bodleian to sign up for reading privileges.

'Are you a member of the university?' the librarian had asked him.

'Yes, I'm the Eastman visiting professor this year,' he had answered, trying not to sound smug.

He could have spared the effort. 'Oh?' she had replied. It was obvious that she had never heard of the Eastman professorship, which is a chair supported by a trust set up in the 1920s by George Eastman of Kodak fame and occupied annually by a distinguished American scholar. 'Well, I'm afraid I shall have to ask you to take the pledge,' she said.

He had done so, hand raised as when giving the Scout Oath:

'I hereby undertake not to abstract from the Library, nor to mark, deface, or injure in any way, any volume, document, or other object belonging to it; nor to bring into the Library or kindle therein any fire or flame, and not smoke in the Library; and I promise to obey all the regulations of the Library.'

Then the librarian had handed over a long printed form, saying, 'Now, will you be good enough to fill out this application?'

As George had sighed and had got out his pen, she'd had a second thought. 'I don't suppose you are by chance a member of a college?'

'Why, yes. I'm a Fellow of Balliol.'

She had hurriedly retrieved the form. 'Oh, I *am* sorry, sir. I didn't understand. In that case, you need not fill out the application.'

He thought that incident was funny, and in following days brought home other bits and pieces of information revealing how

wrong we were to have assigned the colleges a subsidiary rôle in
the university.

'Guess what, honey? I found out today that the university
can't admit any students. That's the prerogative of the colleges.
What's more, they don't have to report to any central agency
how many they have accepted in any given field. Believe it or not,
the Prof didn't have any notion of how many undergraduates
were going to turn up in botany this term until they actually
arrived at the lab!'

Later: 'I was chatting with Mr Bennett at College today. He
says that the university doesn't have a purchasing department,
and that each college bursar buys the small quantities he needs
of staples like light bulbs and paper goods and cleaning supplies.
I asked Mr Bennett if anyone had ever suggested joint purchasing in large quantities in order to save money, and he said he
believed that such a scheme *had* been proposed once but that
nothing seemed to have come of it.'

And also: 'I don't see how this can be true, even at Oxford,
but here's how I heard it. The Botanical Garden— you know, the
buildings and grounds along the Cherwell just below Magdalen
Bridge—is owned by Magdalen College, and they lease it to the
university. Somewhere in the deed or lease there's a provision
forbidding vehicles to drive on to the property. And for a solid
week during one cold winter, while the supply of coal to heat the
greenhouses dwindled away to nothing, Magdalen refused to let
the university deliver coal—because it had to come by truck!'

George's attitude toward the preservation of such individual
liberties ceased to be one of detached amusement, however, after
he'd sampled the Oxford library system. It was, in fact, on the
same day that I came home all steamed up about 'the charm and
quaintness' of the undergraduates at their matriculation ceremony that George paused at home only long enough to slam
down some books and announce that he was going up to the post
office to send a cable to Pasadena.

'What for?' I asked.

'I want the lab at home to air-mail the August *Proceedings of
the National Academy of Sciences*,' he snapped. 'It's buried so
deep in the Bodleian, or the Radcliffe, or *somewhere*, that they
probably won't find it until Christmas.'

There are over fifty libraries at Oxford, some maintained by the university, some by the colleges, some by departments. Cataloguing systems vary from library to library, and sometimes even within them. There is no central catalogue that lists what's supposed to be in all, and such lists as are available are often out of date. In trying to run down one periodical, listed at two department libraries, George had found that one of the two had stopped subscribing to the magazine in question in 1933, and the other had sold its back copies during a period of economic pinch. He still talks about the fact that to locate all reference material pertinent to a survey of evolution required visits to seventeen libraries.

This sort of thing doesn't bother a lot of people at Oxford. Some have more fun sampling their way through the Bodleian than women at what the English call a jumble sale. A copyright library, like the Library of Congress, the Bodleian is a repository for every book that's been printed in Great Britain for hundreds of years. One friend reported with great glee that he'd come upon *The Life and Times of Mickey Mouse* there. But George is a do-it-now person, a lover of efficiency, and to the end of our stay in Oxford he marvelled that so many people do get good research done there.

Nor did he—essentially a transient, especially as Oxford reckons time—ever feel the sense of close kinship to the others in his college that is the basis of the pride with which Englishmen knot their old school ties. The Fellows of Balliol were very kind, but he *was* a Supernumerary Fellow—that is, he could attend college meetings and voice opinions, but could not vote. That privilege had been withdrawn after Felix Frankfurter, an early Eastman professor, had scared the Fellows half to death by participating vigorously in college business.

George went on to one college meeting and came home amused and exhausted. 'I don't know enough college or university politics to understand what they're talking about,' he explained, 'and they swallow half their syllables when they speak, so I don't even hear all the words. They pause and breathe in the middle of the sentence, rush past the period at the end, and pause again in the middle of the next sentence.' He grinned. 'If only I could learn to do it too, I'd sure be able to keep the floor in meetings at home. Nobody would know when to interrupt.'

Thereafter he used the college more as a club than as a headquarters. He lunched and dined there often, but otherwise he was content to remain a Supernumerary. (He delightedly found the word defined in the Oxford Dictionary as 'an extra person engaged for odd jobs'.) His heart was really in the lab, anyway; the atmosphere there was more familiar.

Oxford undergraduates specializing in science take courses comparable to those an American college student would take, with the core of instruction centred in the laboratory rather than in the library. This sets them apart from people in the humanities, a small enough cleavage in itself, but one that is deepened by scientists' careless observation of certain hallowed Oxford rituals—the wearing of academic gowns to lectures or tutorials, for example, and by the fact that scientists (as in the United States) are currently the fair-haired boys in academic circles. It isn't easy for the arts-and-letters people (who dominate the colleges) to see modern science usurping so much of the attention—and, more cruelly, the money—that once went to divinity schools and to Greek scholars. One can hardly blame some of them for hoping that, if they ignore science, maybe it'll go away.

Oxford undergraduates, regardless of their field of specialty, are not required to attend any of the formal lectures scheduled in great abundance for the general edification of anyone who wishes to come. These were the sort that George was to give, and he was as nervous as a cat in March on the first Thursday of Michaelmas term, when he was to make his debut.

Vivian Galbraith, a retired Oxford professor of history—peppery and Puckish at seventy-plus—had spent some time in Pasadena the year before we came to Oxford, and he had heard George give a Caltech lecture on heredity. Intended for the general public, it was long on simple illustrations and short on scientific jargon.

'That's it! That's it!' Professor Galbraith had said. 'That's what you must give them at Oxford. You'll have a crowd the first time, of course—one always does. But if you want them to come back—not that many *will*, you understand, and you are not to take offence, it's just that they *don't*—why, give them a show!'

Roger Mackenzie, on the other hand, had advised something solid and meaty. 'If you could bring us up to date on what Crick is doing with DNA . . .'

'But he's at Cambridge. Surely at Oxford they know what *he's* doing?' George had interrupted.

'Don't count on it,' Roger had replied. 'And I hear Kornberg is getting some amazing results with *in vitro* synthesis; and Meselson—he's your chap at Caltech, isn't he?—has something interesting going on with density gradients.'

As a result of this advice George faced his first audience in a state of some confusion. Then he had a flash of inspiration. Looking up from the lectern, he announced, 'I propose, ladies and gentlemen, to lecture American style.'

It was a good lecture, Cyril Darlington said afterward—solid and meaty, but presented with enough showmanship to keep the audience awake. However, it didn't depart in any significant particular from the standard academic format, which is international. On the way out of the lecture hall the Prof said to George, 'What did you mean by that "American style"?'

'Not a thing,' George cheerfully replied. 'I was just protecting myself in case anything went wrong.'

The university year is divided into three eight-week terms, named in accordance with the Anglican calendar: Michaelmas Hilary, and Trinity. Michaelmas term was the hardest one for us, of course, because we had so much to learn. Like many Americans now abroad, we were anxious to 'do the right thing' in a foreign country, but Oxford academic society a) has so many rules that hardly anyone knows them all; b) permits wide latitude in their observance; and c) assumes that a gentleman will *sense* which rules he may overlook and which ones only a cad would ignore. So we had to feel our way.

Oxonians are very sociable. They pack all their entertaining into Term, the long intervening vacations being used for gathering strength for the next go-around. And Michaelmas term, because it follows the longest vacation and is the start of the academic year, has the giddiest whirl.

A spate of sherry parties began it for us. They were indistinguishable from cocktail parties in the United States, except that waiters passed decanters of sherry—'Dry or sweet, madam?' —instead of martinis. Cocktails aren't commonly served in Oxford; hard liquor (meaning scotch or gin, bourbon being unknown in England) is too expensive. Nor do the English have the highball habit. On those few occasions when cocktails were offered by a host wise in the ways of Americans, he couldn't force himself to recognize our barbaric tastes to a greater extent than by the addition of *one* ice cube to the glass.

'How are you liking England?' a bearded gentleman with leather patches on the sleeves of his tweed jacket would ask.

'Just fine,' I'd reply.

'You'll be missing your steam heating by now, I expect.'*

At first I went to the trouble of explaining that Californians don't have steam heat, and in fact tend to keep their houses rather cool. But I soon gave up. The sceptical eyebrow and the rising 'Hmm?' are well-honed English social weapons. So I'd shift to the weather.

'It hasn't been so very cold yet,' I'd say. 'Just rather wet.'

It had been, too: showers nearly every day, with the luggage in our closets having to be regularly checked for mildew, and the spongy stone in our house soaking up water from the earth so the wallpaper was chronically wet a foot or two above the baseboards. One good thing, though—I never had to sprinkle 'dry' laundry before ironing it.

'Yes, filthy weather, isn't it?' my partner would say. 'Wettest year in my memory. We had no summer at all.'

Then we'd drift off into the crowd, and I'd find myself face to face with a lady I hadn't met. I'd give her my name and ask for hers. She'd tell me, and add, 'Now of course you'll remember it. You Americans are so *good* at names.'

(Not all of us. At the end of our time in Oxford one woman who had made this comment at an early sherry party told me gently that her name is Thompson. I'd been calling her Mrs Johnson all year.)

People who remember names by word association are in trouble when it comes to the heads of Oxford colleges, because they are addressed by title, and many have the same title. I never met both the Rectors—of Exeter and Lincoln—but the one I knew was not a very clerical type. Nor could I associate 'Warden' with the friendly, forthright, easygoing head of Rhodes House, where Rhodes scholars are looked after. Oriel has a Provost, and so has Queen's; Balliol and University have Masters; Magdalen and Corpus Christi have Presidents; Somerville and the other

* Americans like their rooms boiling hot.

women's colleges have Principals; and Christ Church has a Dean. One says, 'Good evening, Master' or, 'I was saying to the Warden just the other day . . .' And if one is new to Oxford, it is quite possible to get through an entire year without ever hearing a head of college identified by name. We were well into spring—and had once been a guest in his own house—before we knew that the Vice-Chancellor (of the university), who was also the President (of Magdalen), was T. S. R. Boase.

Oxford's social etiquette, like so much else in the town, is Victorian. One doesn't telephone an invitation; one writes it. Also the reply. I can recall only one telephoned invitation to an important dinner party, and that was necessitated, the hostess said, by the fact that the date was so close. The date was actually three weeks hence—long enough in California to plan and invite people to a wedding.

The first time I opened an invitation and noted the phrase '7.45 for 8.00 p.m.', I was baffled. I now think that this uniquely English convention is a boon to mankind that should rank with the Magna Carta, marmalade, and madrigals, and I wish it could be exported to America. What the phrase means is this: If you want a glass of sherry before dinner you are expected to arrive at 7.45. Dinner will be served at eight. What's more, dinner *is* served at eight. Nobody has sat around for an hour and a half drinking spirits and eating peanuts. Guests come to table not only sober but with an appetite. What a bonus for the cook!

One day in October, Kitty Turnbull dropped by to take me to a meeting of the Wives' Fellowship—I was in the process of joining every organisation that stretched out even a tentative hand of welcome—and I showed her my note of acceptance to a dinner party to be given by the Vice-Chancellor. 'Is this OK?' I asked. 'The form, I mean?' I had written:

Professor and Mrs G. W. Beadle
accept with pleasure
the kind invitation of the Vice-Chancellor . . .

duplicating, as is correct in the United States, the form of the invitation.

Kitty wrinkled her brow. 'Why, of course,' she said. 'That will do very well. However, there is *another* way of doing it, too.'

Thereafter I acknowledged formal invitations properly: 'Professor and Mrs G. W. Beadle accept with pleasure the kind invitation of . . .' running the phrases together into a solid block.

On the night of the Vice-Chancellor's party, as George was zipping me into my evening dress, he suddenly paused and exclaimed, 'Oh, my gosh! My gown is at Balliol.'

'What difference does that make?'

' "At functions attended by the Vice-Chancellor, members of the university will wear academic gowns",' he intoned. 'University rule.'

'But this isn't an official university function,' I protested. 'It's social. Surely people wouldn't wear academic gowns over *tuxedos?*'

Completely unsure, we decided to seek advice from the porter at the Vice-Chancellor's college. Oxford legend has it that college porters know everything. This one assured us that the occasion *was* social, and that gowns were not required. But when we arrived at the Vice-Chancellor's lodgings and his manservant opened the door, his mask slipped a bit. We noted a small twitching of muscles around his mouth.

'Should I be wearing a gown?' George hazarded.

Jeeves murmured that it was customary.

George said he'd drive over to Balliol and get his gown.

Jeeves pointed out that it was almost eight o'clock. In Oxford one is never tardy—that's one of the inflexible rules—and to have gone for the gown would have made us late.

At this point my eye lit on a table in the foyer. It was piled with academic gowns. 'How about my husband wearing one of those?' I asked. Jeeves gave his permission.

Properly garbed, George mounted the stairs and we greeted the Vice-Chancellor. But the joke was too good to keep, so George promptly confessed that he was wearing one of his hosts gowns. The Vice-Chancellor was amused and genial. 'Watch as the other guests arrive,' he said. 'Half the men will be wearing gowns, and half will ignore the rule.'

He was exactly right. Of the four other men, two had gowns and two did not. One of these latter, the new professor of medicine, hadn't even heard of the rule. It impressed him no end, he said, that George had so quickly mastered Oxford etiquette.

The Oxford colleges, having mostly been built before the eighteenth century, lack certain amenities—handily located bathrooms, for instance—but by way of recompense possess the kind of silver that few Americans ever see outside a museum. Thus they set a table that is visually so satisfying it doesn't much matter what the food tastes like, especially when it is served with first-rate wines.

An elegant English dinner menu, such as the college serve, has a Victorian flavour: soup course, fish course, joint of beef or lamb and three vegetables, a pudding or pastry of some sort (never cake or ice cream), fresh fruit, and cheese with crackers. If it's a private party, such as the Vice-Chancellor's, and ladies are present, the ladies leave the table, powder their noses, and drift into the drawing-room. In ten minutes or so the men come along. Coffee—strong and bitter-black—is served demitasse. In order to kill the taste it is customary to pour in sugar and hot milk. Liqueurs or port may follow. (Also, some hours later, a need for bicarbonate of soda.)

English academic society puts on full dress much more often than its American equivalent. If a dinner invitation does not specify 'informal', guests assume that black ties will be worn. Young ladies then wear short formals, and old ladies wear floor-length dinner dresses. If the invitation specifies 'orders and decorations', men climb into white-tie-and-tails, young ladies shift to ball gowns, and old ladies add white kid gloves and tiaras to their floor-length dinner dresses.

It was at an orders-and decorations dinner given by the Royal Society in London that George met a challenge with more serious implications than being caught at the Vice-Chancellor's without a gown. We had decided to stay overnight at a hotel in the city, hence had brought our evening clothes into town with us. George had rented a full-dress suit in Oxford, supposedly complete with accessories; his distress can be imagined when, upon opening the box, he discovered that no suspenders had been included. Since full-dress trousers have no belt loops, he *was* in a pickle.

I giggled—which, under the circumstances, was most unkind —and offered to run a chain of safety pins all around his waistband, pinning through his shirt and anchoring his trousers to his shorts.

'Very funny,' he muttered, and went to the phone. 'Is the porter on duty, and may I speak to him, please?' he asked. Then, 'Hello. Porter? By any chance is there an extra pair or suspen— er, *braces*, in the hotel? I've just discovered that I left mine in

Oxford, and there isn't any other way to hold up my pan—er, *trousers*. What? Yes, evening dress. You'll inquire? Thank you very much.'

In a few minutes the room buzzer sounded, The porter stood outside, empty-handed.

'I'm sorry, sir,' he said. 'There don't seem to be spare bryces anywhere in the 'ouse. But do you 'appen to 'ave a belt, sir? I'd be 'appy to 'ave you use mine, sir, if I could 'ave the use of your belt.'

So the switch was made. George's belt held up the porter's trousers that evening, and the porter's braces went to the Royal Society dinner. They were maroon with blue and gold stripes, and the only difference between George and the O.B.E.s, O.M.s, and K.G.s in attendance was that everyone could see their decorations.

I didn't go to many such dinners. All-male banquets—even with white ties required—are not uncommon in England, and, of course, in Oxford itself the best feasts are those given by the colleges. They take place in Hall, where women may not dine. That's another of the unbreakable rules. A woman undergraduate tries it just about every year, is caught, and is 'sent down'. The Fellows might make an exception for the Sovereign, but for no lesser woman; which reminds me of a story.

A couple of years ago a new official at the American Embassy in London was invited to dine at one of the colleges and brought his wife along. I suppose they had not read the invitation carefully; goodness knows, it took *me* a while to discard my American-bred assumptions of togetherness and start reading invitations carefully to see whether the pleasure of my company was being requested along with Professor Beadle's.

Anyway, there they were—the invited guest and his uninvited wife. Faced by such a *fait accompli*, it never occurred to the head of the college to have an extra place set for the lady. He simply parked her at his lodgings with his wife. Having gotten all dolled up and driven out from London for a black-tie dinner at one of the famous Oxford colleges with all those fascinating dons, the American wife was doubtless tickled pink to find herself sharing a family dinner with another woman and four small children. Women do not dine in Hall, and that's that.

The glamorous titles of the banquets to which George was

invited—the Boar's Head dinner, the Needle and Thread Dinner, the St Simon and St Jude Dinner, a Christ Church Gaudy—filled me with envy, nor was it dispelled afterward when I let my eyes run over the printed menu and feasted vicariously on six courses and seven wines. It wasn't that I was lonely, eating chops at the kitchen table with Red. It was a simple case of nose-out-of-joint. The one I most wished I had been invited to was a dinner to celebrate (it said on the invitation) 'the 350th anniversary of Sir Davenant's 52nd birthday and his happy release from the Tower after his fourth imprisonment therein, and to drink to the health of the Swan of Isis.'

You can get quite a bit of mending done, or letter writing, on those empty evenings when your husband is dining in college. The radio keeps you company until, at tenish, you decide to go to bed with a book. This keeps you occupied until elevenish, when you turn out the light. Just as you are getting drowsy, Himself comes home. And *then* things hum! He bounds up the stairs and into the bedroom. He flings his topcoat onto a chair. He bounces his shoes into the closet. He smells of Corona Coronas. The port was vintage, he says. It is obvious that he has done it more than justice. The roast beef was jolly good. The Brie was admirable. Old Barclay was in top form tonight. Good chap, Old Barclay, listen to this. . . .

For ten minutes, then, a spirited monologue flows over the head of his supine mate. Finally the contented diner-out stretches, yawns, pats his middle, and climbs into bed. That's when he remembers his manners. 'And what did *you* do tonight, dear?' he inquires politely. If she's a good English wife, she doesn't tell him. If she's an American transplant, she does. The telling does her a lot of good, and doesn't disturb him, because he's already asleep.

There are only two courses of action open to Oxford wives: either stay home and sizzle or make a substitute social life for themselves.

One woman I met, whose husband is now at an English university without the college system, is still sizzled. 'Once a year,' she recalls, 'we wives were privileged to go to the Master's Lodge, were given an ersatz cup of coffee and a bun, and were allowed to look through a peephole at our husbands in Hall below, feasting on the fat of the land.'

She had been corrupted by residence in the United States and Australia, however, so perhaps the more typical wife is the one who said to me, 'Oxford wives have a life of their own. It is quite as stimulating in its way as that of our husbands.' She said this most firmly, and since she had been in Oxford thirty years to my one, I should not even now dispute her. Perhaps, as with so much at Oxford, the satisfactions of a separate social life increase with age.

One thing I *did* learn; you can't beat City Hall. The colleges set a better table than any woman can, and the after-dinner conversation of fellow-scholars in a senior common room is likely to be more interesting than the domestic trivia of a wife's day. So the successful Oxford wife is the one who early accepts her husband's college as his mistress.

Chapter 6

THE HEAD of an Oxford college tells this story:

After he had given a public lecture, a little lady bustled up to him and enthused, 'Oh, Master, that was splendid! Your topic was a subject about which I have always been so confused!'

Pleased, he said, 'And now you understand it better?'

'Not really,' she replied, 'but I'm confused on a much higher level.'

That's how a newcomer to Oxford feels as he tries to get the organization of the university straight in his head, and I dare say that's the effect our explanations had on our first visitor from home, Janet Lindvall. Being with us was more pleasant for her than to roam around by herself while her engineer husband was in Russia on an official visit. And her coming was wonderful for us, because it gave us a chance to show off all our newly acquired knowledge.

Essentially, we told her, the university is not unlike the United States of America, especially during that period when we were governed by the Articles of Confederation, and is just as subject to confusion, inefficiency, and jurisdictional disputes as the federal government and any of its sovereign states.

The university has no permanent head, in the sense that American universities have presidents. (And no trustees, either. Faculties of European universities are horrified that Americans not only allow but actually encourage *businessmen* to set policy for academic institutions.) Oxford's official head is its Chancellor, a noted citizen who serves for life but takes no active part in university affairs and is recognized by all as a figurehead. Such leadership as the university actually gets is provided by the heads of colleges, who take on the job of Vice-Chancellor in rotation, for two-year terms each. The only source of administrative continuity, therefore, is provided by the Registrar, a paid officer; and a host of advisory or legislative bodies. These have the advantages and disadvantages of government committee anywhere.

The largest of these bodies is Convocation, a group composed
of all graduates with M.A. or higher degrees—some sixteen
thousand people, scattered all over the world. Naturally, only a
fraction of them is ever on hand to consider university business.
But they have the *right*. Some years back, when the university
proposed to eliminate an entrance examination of a religious
nature, elderly clergymen crept out of retirement all over the
British Isles and converged on Oxford in order to vote against
the proposal. All that defeated them was a last-ditch appeal, by
proponents of the resolution, to those younger members of Convocation known to have a more 'modern' viewpoint. In London
the City was pretty well emptied on the day Convocation voted
to eliminate the religious exam.

In practice day-to-day decisions of the university are made by
dissolving Convocation into a smaller body called Congregation.
This group, composed of those who are actively at work in the
university, numbers about a thousand. And *it* elects the eighteen
members of the Hebdomadal Council (delicious name!), who
really run the university. More or less, that is; one of the first
lessons one learns at Oxford is that nothing is exact. There is
also a body called the Curators of the Chest, who control the
university purse strings. It has equal status with the Hebdomadal
Council. The only way to resolve a stalemate between them is to
appeal to Congregation.

In short, it takes a long time and a lot of talk to get anything
done at Oxford. It is so decentralized, and individual liberties
are so jealousy guarded, that nobody knows for sure what anybody else is doing—at either the college or the university level.
To emphasize this point, George told Janet how, many years
ago, Balliol had acquired a house for the use of the Eastman
professor.

'It needed fixing up,' he said, 'and Balliol split the responsibility between the two bursars. The domestic bursar had charge
of the house interior, and the estates bursar had charge of the
house exterior. Well, when the job was done and the bills were
rendered, the domestic bursar decided to have a look at what he
was paying for. The biggest single item of expense had been the
paintwork inside the conservatory—and guess what? He discovered that after his men had done their painting the men
hired by the estates bursar had torn the conservatory down!'

Janet dissolved in laughter. 'You're making it up!'

'Well, it was told me as a fact. And it certainly *could* have happened. Oxford is that kind of place. No strong central administration, thirty-five autonomous colleges that intend to stay that way,* operation by conference and committee.'

We had explained the tutorial system to her, and the dual social-instructional role of the colleges, but she didn't understand how university appointments fitted into the picture. Janet is a long-time member of the League of Women Voters and likes to get all the facts.

'You introduced me to Professor Darlington the other day, when you took me to the lab,' she said, 'and you told me that he's the head of the Botany Department. That's *university*, isn't it? All right. And he told me that his college is Magdalen. Does that mean that Magdalen appoints the head of the Botany Department?'

'No,' said George. 'Well, yes, in a way. The professorship carries with it a fellowship at Magdalen, so the college has a voice in choosing the professor. But the actual appointment is made by the university.

'Professorships are rare appointments, though,' he continued. 'Let's take a more typical example—the appointment of a reader or a demonstrator, someone equivalent to our assistants and associates at home. Suppose the Faculty of Physical Sciences, which includes chemists and physicists, regardless of their college affiliations, should decide that more-up-to-date instruction in nuclear physics ought to be offered. Suppose, too, that the Faculty Board believes that Dr So-and-So is the best man for the job.

'They could go ahead and make him an offer, but since a man doesn't have much status at Oxford without a college affiliation, the first effort of a Faculty Board is to try to find a college willing and able to take him on as a tutor. It is also nice for the university budget to have a college pay part of such a man's salary.

'Naturally, since he will be closely associated with them socially, the Fellows of the college will be interested in what

* The year after we were at Oxford a new Chancellor had to be elected by members of the university. One reason that Sir Oliver Franks, an Oxford resident, lost out to Prime Minister Harold Macmillan was that Franks would be too close. The dons felt that he might take too seriously the opportunity to provide administrative leadership for the university.

kind of a person the candidate *is*, as well as in what he knows about the atom. They'll give due weight, of course'—and here George grinned—'to the fact that part of the man's salary will be paid by the university.

'But let's suppose that this particular college has a majority of Fellows whose hearts belong to the humanities, and also a big enough endowment so they can afford to be independent. They might say to the Faculty of Physical Sciences that there are quite enough science chaps around the college already and that what they really want is a man who knows something about Plutarch.

'So,' George continued, 'the Faculty of Physical Sciences will then start all over, and try to ease its nuclear physicist into Oxford life via *another* college. And at the same time, mind you, the Faculty of Theology may be hunting a spot for a specialist on liturgies, and the Faculty of Modern History may be trying to place an expert on constitutional law, and some of the colleges may be trying to wangle university jobs for men *they'd* like to hire.

'In the end, of course, if none of these deals work out, and either the university or a college is convinced that it has to have a certain man, it hires him. Colleges have been known to hire tutors despite the fact that the professor in the same field of specialty has said he won't have the man in his department under any circumstances.'

Janet thought it all over. 'I believe the story about the Eastman professor's house,' she decided. 'If so much business at Oxford is done by conferences and committees, people here must just hate to write memos or check with anybody they don't absolutely *have* to.'

I had been invited to a luncheon during the time of Janet's visit and telephoned my hostess to ask if it would be possible to bring my guest. Mrs Ward-Spencer was delighted. 'Mrs Sutherland is among those who are coming,' she remarked. 'Have you met Mrs Sutherland yet? You haven't? She rather collects Americans. And now'—there was a ring of triumph in her voice—'I've got two!'

There was a lot of talk that day about the progress of construction on a new by-pass road just outside Oxford. The theory was that it would relieve the heavily congested streets in the city centre by, in particular, diverting heavy traffic bound from the south of England to the industrial north—but the ladies were not at all sure it would.

'That's what they said about the Southern By-Pass,' Mrs Sutherland remarked (to whose credit it should be noted that she had paid no undue attention to either Janet or me). 'But as far as I can see, it's stickier than ever around the Carfax.'

'My husband has completely given up driving to work,' I said. 'He can't stand the traffic. So he walks.'

'He *walks*?' exclaimed Mrs Ward-Spencer. 'From Headington? It's two miles.'

'He follows the footpaths, and angles across the country, so it really isn't that far,' I said. 'And it's terribly pretty. He's especially fond of the ducks, and all those willowy clumps along the river.'

'He walks,' Mrs Sutherland repeated in tones of wonder. 'How very un-American.'

Oxford is like Boston: it's got itself backed into such a tight corner that the only practical solution would seem to be for the city fathers to tear it all down and start over. Only of course they can't, partly because such a course would in itself be a decision, and all they have been willing to do for the past ten or fifteen years is to talk; and partly because the easy way to achieve an efficient street plan and an orderly flow of traffic would require the partial destruction of some of the city's finest historical monuments. And not even the most ruthlessly progressive American could justify street widening that would eliminate the seventeenth-century baroque porch on St Mary the Virgin Church, or damage that charming eighteenth-century bottleneck called Holywell Street—just to speed a van full of refrigerators through town. What is needed is a bold and imaginative town planner, someone as dynamic as Robert Moses, and as persuasive as Circe; and it wouldn't hurt at all if he'd taken a First in Greats at the university in his youth and is now known to be keen on association football, a kind of soccer that is highly popular with the working classes. Lacking such a person (and I don't suppose he even exists), the good citizens of Oxford are slowly suffocating in their own exhaust fumes.

Janet was surprised by the prevailing Victorian architecture of Oxford. I had been, too; I suppose the British Travel Association ads were at fault, for they emphasize thatched-roof cottages, half-

timbered fourteenth-century inns, and Scottish baronial castles.
If one expects buildings that are either quaint or magnificent,
it's a shock to come face to face with so many great, gaunt mauso-
leums of polychromatic brick, each with as much gingerbread
decoration (in stone, rather than band-sawed wood) as any Midwest Gothic.

However, even these are not typical. The most usual house in
Oxford or elsewhere in English Midlands cities is a tall, narrow,
brick duplex, each side with two bay windows up and two bay
windows down, all of them angular and graceless. For some ob-
scure reason such houses are called 'semi-detached'. I have never
seen two halves of a peach more closely joined, but the individual
owners treat each half as if the other half were miles away. It is
not uncommon to see the wood trim on one side of such houses
painted orange, with a green door, and that on the other side a
like combination of red and maroon. If the house itself is paint-
able, the walls of each half may be of different colours too. The
paint, incidentally is almost certain to be fresh, the brasswork
on the doors as shiny as daily polishing can make it, and at any
season of the year there is sure to be a potted plant or a bouquet
of flowers behind the spotless windowpanes of the inevitable
bays. The English are house-proud.

They're illogical, too. Against the outer walls of such dwellings
are the water pipes, wholly exposed to the weather and almost
sure to freeze at least once in the course of the winter. I called
a batch of these to Janet's attention as we chugged home toward
Headington after our luncheon party. 'There's a joke about those
exposed pipes,' I said. 'At least six people have told it to me. "Yes,
but when the pipes *do* freeze, they're so easy to get at." '

The two of us made daily pilgrimages to the various colleges.
I took Janet to my favourites, and we ticked off some new ones.
They're all different. In some you feel as if you're strolling
through the grounds of a Stately Home—as at Worcester College,
with its lovely lake; or at Magdalen, which has a deer park,
magnificent gardens, a piece of the river, well-preserved buildings
of uncommon beauty, and so many tourists the undergraduates
have a hard time getting through the gates. In some colleges
time seems to have stood still since some golden moment in history. The Great Hall at Christ Church College is one of those; it
could have been yesterday that Henry VIII dined at High Table

there. In some colleges you are especially aware of the *flow* of time. New College is one such. In its cloisters there are medieval stone saints, an eighteenth-century fire engine, and quantities of flesh-and-blood pigeons: together they distill the essence of a five-hundred-year span into the living present.

'New College?' Janet asked. '*How* new?' (She was getting wise to Oxford ways.)

'Fourteenth century.'

She giggled.

'There are four or five that are older,' I said. 'Incidentally the people who started this one got the land cheap because the victims of the plague had been buried here. When we get into the garden you'll see a nice long bit of the old city wall, and a mound where King Charles mounted his cannon when he was trying to hold out against Cromwell. The cloisters here were used as an arsenal.'

'They're very impressive,' Janet said, pausing to read a plaque to the memory of John Galsworthy. 'But I've been wondering something about Oxford. I suppose even here things wear out and have to be replaced, or additions are required. With the past so—well, not actually pressing down on you, but so *dominant*, however are they going to switch to a more modern style of building? The architecture just won't jibe.'

'I think that's why people here turn their noses up at Nuffield College,' I said. 'That's the new one down by the railroad station, remember? It tries to look like the old colleges, but its lines are more streamlined, and its spire is very modern. Over-all, it's neither fish nor fowl—not good modern, not good eighteenth century. Matter of fact, I haven't seen any really exciting modern design so far in England—it's either too belligerent, like that technical college we pass on the bus when we come into town, or too timid, like Nuffield.'

'Fred and I stopped off at Harvard on our way to England,' Janet said, 'and they've certainly got very *modern* modern mixed in with their old buildings. The campus reminded me of Henry Dreyfuss's contention that if a work of art is good of its period, it'll go well with the best work of other periods.'

'Come on into the chapel here,' I proposed. 'You'll have a chance to see whether you agree with him.'

The Oxford colleges are most dissimilar in their chapels. Christ

Church's is so big it's a small cathedral; in fact, it serves as the cathedral for the city, too. I liked going there because more than any other place in Oxford I could feel the centuries rushing by. The historical journey begins with the sturdy Norman under-pinnings, continues as the eye arrives at the delicately fan-vaulted fifteenth-century ceiling, lingers on the muted greens and blues and careful brushwork of the seventeenth-century windows, zips by the ruby-red and sapphire glass the Victorians installed, and finally comes to rest on yesterday's bouquets, lovingly and art-fully arranged by the ladies of the church guild. Brasenose College has a fan-vaulted ceiling too, but it's been grafted onto wood and painted, and it has a nice air of country freshness. Keble's chapel is a boisterous blending of brick and mosaic. Hertford's has a Quakerish simplicity. And Trinity's is as florid as a fruit-cake. Sometimes, when you steal into one of these darkened interiors, you catch an undergraduate practising on the organ. He pretends that you aren't there, and so do you, and a lovely quarter of an hour ensues.

At New College chapel Janet thought that the Joshua Rey-nolds windows, all in shades of gold and bronze, were as beautiful as I had thought she would, wrinkled her nose at Epstein's very modern, very blocky sculpture called *Lazarus*, also as I had thought she would, and said, 'Ooh!' when she spotted the mass of carved figures (the reredos) behind the altar. But what both of us saw for the first time was a girl on her hands and knees in a corner of the antechapel.

'Is she praying?' Janet whispered, and I couldn't answer, so we eased over to one side to get a view of what she was doing.

The girl had a great sheet of paper laid over one of the brasses, which are tomb ornaments of a type popular in the Middle Ages. They are portraits in one plane of the worthy who lies below them, and are fun to study because they reproduce the actual clothing of their day much more faithfully than stone tomb effigies do. The latter are great on classical drapery but skimpy on detail, and if you want to know how a fourteenth-century knight really looked in mixed mail and plate armour. you have to find the brass engraving that was set into the lid of his coffin.

The brass that the girl was bending over was one showing a bygone don in fifteenth-century academic dress, and she was making an impression of it by rubbing a black waxy ball across the paper she had laid down—just as children 'copy' coins through paper. When she paused to rest, I asked, 'What are you going to do with it when it's done?'

'Hang it in my digs. If it's good enough; this is my third go at it. It takes a bit of practice to maintain an even pressure as one rubs, and the paper shifts rather easily.'

(Subsequently I saw some framed rubbings of brasses. They make handsome room decorations.)

Poor Janet, as the first of our American visitors, got the full treatment—but she was game, and kept asking for more. I took her to the spectacular chapel at All Souls College, which has some famous brasses and a magnificent reredos; the statues in this one, forming a breath-taking backdrop for the altar, are large, well-separated, and in full relief—obviously portraits. I think of them still as 'all the souls of the faithful departed' for whom the college was named. Magdalen's chapel has windows painted in sepia-and-white chiaroscuro, in which the combina-tion of light coming through the glass plus the artist's technique in rendering shadows gives a three dimensional quality to the figures. Exeter's chapel is a little jewel, a miniature St Chapelle, and so is its Fellows' Garden—a tiny sunken garden tucked into a narrow opening between two high and ancient grey stone build-ings, with the classic cupola of the Radcliffe Library and the frilly pinnacles of St Mary's filling the sky beyond it.

The Rector of Exeter is an astute and affable gentleman named Kenneth Wheare. (Along with his wife and son Tom, he gave us exceeding comfort and joy throughout our Oxford year. It is as much the example of their friendship as any other circum-stance that now makes us especially watchful of the welfare of *our* visiting families from overseas.) He tells with great glee of how, one day, he observed a couple of American tourists—a father and twelve-year-old son—wandering around, out of visiting hours, in the Fellows' Garden. The man was taking pictures, and the boy was romping on the grass. Hating to yell at them—conduct un-befitting a Rector—but wishing to register his displeasure at their trespass, he stood at the window of his study, puffing furiously at his pipe, and glared down at them. It was the boy who caught sight of him. Whereupon, he carolled out to his father, 'Hey, Dad, *look*! These ruins are inhabited!'

Exeter, Lincoln, and Jesus colleges lie close together on the quaint little Oxford street called the Turl, all three of them presenting similar façades to the street. It's hard to distinguish one from the others, out of which fact has grown a favourite Oxford joke. A newcomer—American, of course—is alleged to have said, 'I can't tell the difference between Lincoln and Jesus.' His guide replied, 'No American can.'

I paced Janet up to the roof of St Mary's for a view of the colleges from above—the city looks like a leafy bower from that height—and down into the crypt of St Peter-in-the-East, which was built within a hundred years of the Norman Conquest and has probably had a puddle of rain water on the floor ever since. We saw the famous chained books in Merton College library, a nice reminder of the days when books were as precious as jewels and had to be guarded from thieves; and went into the Christ Church kitchen, where the huge fireplaces and spits long enough for a side of beef remain unchanged from the sixteenth century.

The headmaster of Red's school, Robert Stanier, had by now become a person instead of a title, and we had also met his wife, a charming woman who is Oxford's unofficial poet laureate. Under the pen name of Culex her verses appear regularly in the Oxford newspapers and have been reprinted in two small volumes. Toward the end of Janet's stay with us, and after a particularly exhausting day of sight-seeing, I got out *Culex's Guide to Oxford*, flipped it open to a favourite verse, and laid it on Janet's lap. She read:

TOURIST'S ROUND

Marcato con brio Into the Chapel and round the Quad
Up the Turl and down the Broad,
Through the Kitchen and up the Stair,
Hurry on, madam; quicker, sir.

Presto Here's the glove Elizabeth wore,
Mark the genuine Norman door.
This is Cardinal Wolsey's hat.
And that is where the Parliament sat.

Rallentando (I could do with a seat—and how!
Not now, darling, hush, not now!)

Prestissimo Keble's the one that's made of brick.
Magdalen's strong on the perpendic.

> Gilbert Scott on the left, and then
> On the right for Christopher Wren.
> Notice the Epstein on your way,
> Very symbolical, so they say.

Janet smiled, closed the book, wiggled her tired toes, and said, 'Amen!'

'Here's my gamma card,' Red said one evening, handing across the dinner table a sizeable piece of pasteboard labelled 'Position Card.'

'Why "gamma card"?' George inquired.

'That's what the fellows call it. Because the lowest grade is gamma. I didn't get any.' (Was there a trace of smugness in his voice?)

The card was ruled into squares, as American report cards are, with the first three letters of the Greek alphabet replacing the As, Bs, Cs, Ds, and Fs commonly used in the United States. The back of the card provided the key:

α shows that the boy is in the top section of the class

β shows that the boy is in the middle section of the class

γ shows that the boy is in the bottom section of the class

The sign * indicates that a boy has made a commendable effort even if he remains in a low section of the class

The sign $\pm$ indicates that he has not done as well as he should even if he is in a high section

'But, George,' I said. 'That's *comparative* grading. Remember that ruckus at home a couple of years ago? The people who demanded that A must stand for 90, B for 80, and so forth? One of their big talking points was that the English schools have such tough and objective standards of grading.'

George, himself a teacher, brushed that aside. 'You can't give course grades on that basis, anyway. Just exam grades . . . Look here; what interests me is this "set" scheme. If I understand the theory, this starred alpha that Red got in physics ought to mean that he'll be moved up to a higher set so he'll have to work harder.'

Red groaned. We ignored him; it had a ritualistic ring.

'The English have a wonderful word for it,' I said. 'They call it "stretching".'

Sets are ability groups. In each subject the boys had been divided into fast, average and slower-moving sections; each of these sets met as a class. Red was in Set I in English, maths, history, and geography; Set II in Latin and French; and Set III in physics, chemistry, and biology.

His starred alpha in physics indicated that he was doing top work and had made a 'commendable effort' besides. He had also gotten an alpha in Latin. These alphas could promote him to a higher set—to Set II in physics and to Set I in Latin. But he'd gotten a beta in French; it would have to come up to an alpha before he could move to Set I. Conversely, if it dropped to a gamma, he might sink into Set III.

Thus, within a school whose pupils were already highly selected for academic ability, three degrees of competence *in every subject* were recognized—a device that not only made teaching easier, because the boys in a given class were more nearly equal in ability, but also one that rewarded industry and punished laziness in the pupils. It's a fine scheme. It deserves an alpha with *two* stars.

The list of subjects was much longer than Red would have been taking at home. In addition to those listed on his card, he was taking art, physical education, and Scripture—for which no grades were given. The school packed them all into a thirty-six-hour week by varying the number of hours assigned weekly to each subject. Latin, French, and the subject Red now called 'maths' rated five hours each; everything else got less. He had had a choice of Greek, or geography and art in the same time slot; otherwise there were no electives.

At the top of the card the name of Red's 'house'—Wilkinson—appeared. There wasn't any house, in a physical sense; it was a system of organization (borrowed from boarding schools like Eton) that created small fraternal groups within the school. I had at first thought of Red's house, in American terminology, as his home room. But it was far more—a clan, almost. Intramural athletics and other contests were organized as matches between houses. Each had a master whose job it was to keep tabs on the progress and problems of the boys in his group. Since the number of boys in a house didn't exceed seventy-five or eighty, and they remained in the same group throughout their school days, in time the housemaster would get to know them—and vice

versa—really well. The English house system deserves an alpha
with two stars too.

(Some American school districts are now using a variation of
it to create small groups within huge schools, to give pupils a
sense of 'belonging'. For their entire time in high school pupils
are assigned to one specific block of classrooms, with a specific
group of teachers; going out of their school-within-a-school to
labs, shops, auditorium, and cafeteria, which the entire student
body shares in common. It's an excellent way to combat the
impersonality of numbers.)

A few days after the position card had been signed and
returned, George and I set out, as summoned by letter, to a
meeting of the school Parents' Association.

'And I was so pleased to get free of the P.T.A. for a year,' I
remarked, as we picked our way along a pitch-black path toward
the only lighted building on the school grounds.

'Somehow, I think you *are* free of the P.T.A.,' George said as
we entered. He was right: there were as many fathers as mothers
in the audience; the hall was full five minutes *before* the meeting
was scheduled to start; no paper drive was announced; and nobody said a word about Understanding Your Adolescent. It was
all very restful.

The chairman announced that the Christmas Fair the pre-
ceding year had made £160, up £40 from the year before. He
said that Mrs Pye would have charge of it again and that she
needed ladies to help with the teas; in fact he believed that she
would welcome a word after the meeting with any of the ladies
present who wished to offer their services, isn't that correct, Mrs
Pye? A little red-haired woman in the front row bounced to her
feet, nodded vigorously, and beamed at the audience. All around
me, I heard voices murmuring that they'd be delighted to help
out. *This is most certainly not the P.T.A.*, I thought.

It was at this meeting that I learned what a direct-grant school
is. It's a private school that receives tax support (in the form of
a grant directly from the Ministry of Education). In return it
must take up to half its pupils as 'free' boys—mostly those who
have passed the local 11-plus exams with distinction. Other
pupils pay fees as they would at any private school anywhere.
They are admitted at the discretion of the headmaster, or on the
basis of passing exams of his choice. Thus, schools like Magdalen

College School include boys from both upper and lower social classes. (At this very parents' meeting, I caught the 'oi' sound that replaces 'i' in Oxfordshire speech, an accent that will be gone from the voices of their sons by the time they have been exposed to B.B.C. English throughout their school years.)

There aren't many direct-grant schools in Great Britain—fewer than two hundred. They are relics of that pre-1944 period when established private secondary schools were offered tax support as an inducement for taking in bright but poor boys. Now, however, the direct-grant schools compete with the state-supported system of grammar schools, their greater prestige and smaller classes creaming off the most able youngsters. Hence they come under sporadic attack. But their champions defend them because they are 'a blending of rich and poor, and for that reason a bridge between the state schools and the wholly independent schools.'

The history of the direct-grant schools has a parallel in the church schools which, in the nineteenth century, provided all the elementary education there was. It is characteristic of the English, who never discard anything that still works, to have supplemented existing facilities rather than to have created entire new systems, as Americans would have done. Therefore, today, there are church schools (of various faiths, not just Church of England) that get their *operating* expenses from the tax funds, retaining responsibility for capital improvements along with the right to choose their entire teaching staff; and there are other church schools that are supported completely by the taxpayers. In return these have no say in the appointment of teachers, except for the headmaster and the teacher who provides religious instruction. At the two extremes, as in the United States, lie the wholly independent schools and the wholly tax-supported schools. With regard to these latter, it always amused me—recalling bitter fights at home over Released Time for Religious Education or the propriety of reading the Bible in public schools—that English law makes an assembly with prayers mandatory in any school that receives tax money.

By American standards it's a crazy quilt of a school system. We could never make it work; we have too Teutonic a fondness for codification and chains of command. But tolerence, respect for tradition, and a stubborn distrust of centralization have characterized the English for generations. They like cautious experiment rather than radical change, and if this predilection sometimes muddles them up, costs them money, and slows them down, at least it spares them the disillusionment that can follow the collapse of some grandiose but untried scheme.

A couple of weeks after the first Parents' Association meeting at Magdalen College School, we groped our way back—this time in dense fog—to a meeting of Wilkinson House parents. The nearest American equivalent would be a grade-level meeting, but American parents would not have been so deferential in their greetings to the housemaster and his two assistants, who greeted us in black academic gowns and apologized for not being able to offer us a cup of tea on such a damp, chill night.

The purpose of the meeting was to answer parental questions, some of which were as universal as the existence of schoolboys:

'How hard should I press my son in the matter of prep?' a father asked. Answer: 'Be quite strict, but adjust to the boy. If he works fast, and can finish in twenty minutes, don't force him to spend thirty. If it takes him too long, be sure he is spending his time profitably. The most important thing about prep is to make him understand that he's not doing it for Old Mr So-and-So, but for his own sake.'

A mother asked if something couldn't be done to get the boys to bring their damp towels home, instead of letting them mould in their lockers; a father requested that a stern warning be given to those bike riders he'd seen on the streets riding side by side— 'a very dangerous practice'; and another asked what the parents of fifth-formers should be doing, if anything, to plan for their sons' university admission two years hence. In America the answer to that last one would never have been phrased as it was in Oxford. The housemaster began, 'Some Oxford colleges prefer that the boy apply at the end of his penultimate year. . . .'

There were half a dozen American families represented in the group. (This was due in part to the fact that the university draws many foreigners to Oxford, and in part to the fact that Mr Stanier likes Americans. He thinks that they liven things up.) The questions asked by the American parents were of quite a different order from the questions asked by the English parents:

'In determining grades, how much weight do you give to recitation, how much homewor—er, prep, and how much to examinations?' asked a man from Massachusetts. (Home university, Harvard.) The housemaster looked startled. He finally replied that there was no rigid formula

A woman from Illinois (home university, Northwestern) wanted to know what percentage of class time was set aside for conversational French. She finished with, 'What is your policy in this matter?' The housemaster must have fought back a smile —what very *American* questions!—as he answered that the masters were aware that conversational skill was desirable.

In short, the Americans wanted details of curriculum, and the English—as I had already noted at ladies' coffee parties—did not. Did the English refrain because they already knew the answers or because they thought that what the schools teach is none of their business? A little of both, probably. Americans, of course, consider everything that goes on within a school as very much their business. ('We *pay* for them, don't we?')

It was certainly not my intention to alter the genteel tone of the meeting, but the minute I uttered my question I sensed that it was as tactless as mentioning socialized medicine among a group of American doctors. My question was this: 'I've been reading in the papers that there is considerable opposition to the establishment of comprehensive secondary schools such as we have in the United States. Could you tell me why?'

The housemaster flushed slightly. Then he took a breath and replied. 'We in the grammar schools are not opposed to the idea,' he said, 'but we believe that the political pressure to build more comprehensive schools—there are, as you no doubt know, a good many of them in London—is unwise. They have been in existence only ten years, and many of us feel, since they are still experimental, that it is too soon to judge them.

'Secondly, the heart of the grammar school is the individual attention and supervision which it makes possible. The boys have direct contact with the headmaster. I don't see how that would be possible in a school with two thousand children. It *is* the essence of a comprehensive school that it must be large, I believe?'

I nodded. 'Yes, since it includes children of all academic abilities—that is, both those who would go to grammar schools and to secondary modern schools, here. Unless there is a large group to draw from, it's impossible to find enough pupils of the

same academic ability to make course offerings sufficiently
varied.'

The housemaster continued. 'Many of us are not at all sure
but what the academic-minded boys would be held back by the
presence of the others. It is our experience in the grammar
schools that individual progress depends on the homogeneity of
the group. Slow boys would be bewildered if put in a fast group,
and of course fast boys would be held back by the slow.'

I opened my mouth to argue—well, at least to *clarify*—the
point, since the academic-minded pupils in most American high
schools take academic courses, and the slow pupils don't; but
George put a cautionary hand on my arm, and I remained silent.

'Finally,' the housemaster said, 'it's the same principle that
causes one to send a promising musician to a music academy
rather than to a village choir. Since the future of our country
depends on brains, many of us believe that our job is to find and
train those intelligences which will be capable of the judgment
we need for the nation's future welfare. And the grammar
schools seem to do this job exceedingly well.'

He was dangerously close to an un-English show of emotion,
and his audience was so stirred they spontaneously applauded.
I murmured a meek 'thank you'. Flustered by having allowed
himself to be carried away, the housemaster cleared his throat,
smiled apologetically, and remarked, 'I'm afraid it's become a
political plank.'

I didn't find out until later that the London comprehensive
schools are the work of a Labour-dominated city council that
has built them as much (or maybe more) for social as for educational reasons. Since the present system of segregated schools
helps to maintain class distinctions, England's socialists hope to
eliminate such distinctions by establishing comprehensive
schools throughout the country. You can hardly blame the class
that is being eliminated for objecting.

It is a widespread assumption in England that the academic-
ally most able children cannot be well educated in comprehensive
schools; I am not at all certain that anyone really believed me
when I told them that we *do* put children of varying ability into
specialized groups. The educated Englishman's other fear of the
comprehensive school, however, is justified. The outward mark
of education is good speech. The educated Englishman fears that

the distinctive accent and discriminating word choice at present built into the élite 20 per cent of school children would be blurred and diluted by everyday contact with the other 80 per cent. And he's right.

Personally, I think that day is coming. But as of now, quoting an Oxford headmaster, 'Speech matters. Oh, how it *does* matter!' Or, quoting an Australian scientist newly come to Oxford, 'I've no liking for class schools, so I tried sending my boy to the neighbourhood state school. He's begun to speak with an Oxfordshire accent. Well, his future is in England. I've no right to handicap him. Next term, he's going to a private school'. You see? No neutral position is possible.

Chapter 7

ENGLAND had been green and glowing with bloom when we arrived. Gardens were bright with dahlias, daisies, and delphiniums. The rain would knock their petals off and bend them to earth, but every morning they'd be upright again, full of fresh bud and blossom. Lawns and meadows were pure plush, and it was like being in ocean depths to look up from below at the rich dark canopy of green that linked the trees together.

Then the chestnut leaves had begun to turn and fall; a few drifters at first, but by late October a bronze carpet lay across the paths in the parks. The sun rose later every day, blood-red through low-lying mists. The lush green of the countryside began to grey, a milky wash suffused the blue of the sky, and even at midday the air had a smoky haze.

On such a day we set out for Stratford-on-Avon. We were tired of people, tired of sherry parties, tired of tossing tidbits of news to each other when we happpened to meet on our own doorstep. Deciding that our family batteries needed recharging, we'd gotten tickets for *Hamlet,* and now, a little after noon, we were ready to go.

'Red roads, or yellow?' George inquired. 'Yellow!' Red and I chorused—meaning that we wanted to travel on the secondary roads, which are yellow on the map. These are the roads that take one to places with marvellous rolling names like Wooton-under-Edge, Weston-super-Mare, Fifehead St Quinton, and Norton-juxta-Twycross. There are lots of other Nortons: East, King's, Pudding, Brize, and Cold (to name a few); and almost as many Bartons: Steeple, Upper, Nether, Earls, and Abbot's. Sometimes the neat little country signposts made us snicker; names like Lower Swell, Little Crawley, and Great Snoring were always popping up. But whenever we got to thinking that English place names were just too droll for words, we could count on Red's reminding us of American towns like Down Sockum and Truth or Consequences. Then he'd dig into the Ekwall dictionary of place-names, and together they'd peel the centuries back like the layers of an onion. English place-names are living relics of changing languages and ownership over the course of a thousand years, and we never passed through towns like Stretton-on-Fosse or Duntisborne Rouse without learning some history.

(O.K., since you ask: The Old English word for 'Roman road' was *straet*, and a town on a Roman road was a *straettun*. One of the famous ancient roads of Britain led south-west from Lincoln to Bath, and was distinctive because of the *fossa*, or ditch, alongside it. A hamlet in what was to become Warwickshire therefore distinguished itself from other towns on Roman roads by identifying itself as the one on the road by the ditch. As for Duntisborne Rouse, a good many invaders of England march through one's mind as one ponders its name. In Saxon times, it was a place by Dunt's *burne*, or steam; with the Norman Conquest it passed into new hands. In the thirteenth century a Roger le Rus held it—his family name already evolving from the French *roux* that had described some forebear's hair.)

The yellow roads, and the towns they led to, always yielded some small delight. Often it was a sign announcing the presence nearby of an Ancient Monument, which always brought George braking to a stop and sent the lot of us scrambling up a muddy lane to gaze at a Long Barrow or a circle of lichen-encrusted stones dating from 1500 B.C. Once we had stopped in the town of Cricklade just as the children were queuing up for their harvest service at the church, their little arms strained around giant cabbages or already-wilting bunches of daisies to take to the altar. In Cirencester two waiters had fallen into a quarrel while advising us whether the town's name should be correctly pronounced Cisseter or Cissester. (It was there we first saw the shop sign 'Carpenter, Joiner, and Undertaker' and suddenly realized that England is blessedly free of mortuaries.) In Lower Slaughter we had met three geese as rapacious as the bears in Yellowstone, as well as an itinerant blacksmith who had showed us a horseshoe made in the fifteenth century. 'And a proper prize it is,' he said. 'The Victoria an' Albert 'ave offered two quid for it.' He kept it wrapped in velvet in the back of his rattletrap truck.

So on this Saturday in October we set out for the north with high hopes. We were not disappointed. Just beyond Woodstock we came up behind a gypsy caravan, and in due course eased

THESE RUINS ARE INHABITED

past it. The entourage, in the order in which each unit came
into view, included a lithe young boy riding bareback on a rangy
little pony; a pony-drawn cart whose paintwork was gay with
flowers and scrolls; and, at the head of the procession, a brand-
new house trailer. It was peacock blue and white, and its chrome
trim sparkled in the sun. So did the bangles on the bridles of
the horses that were pulling it. Walking alongside was the head
of the family, a short, swart man wearing gold earrings, denim
Levis, and sneakers. As an Oxford don might put it, *tempora
mutantur, et nos mutamur in illis.*

Not far from Shipston-on-Stour, in a green bowl of meadows
and woodland, we found Compton Wynyates, its mellow pink
brick dyed red by the setting sun.

'The chimneys,' I said as we shuffled up the gravelled drive,
our half-crowns ready for the caretaker's little black box. 'Look
at those spiralled chimneys. Like fluted candles.'

'This place is Elizabethan?' George asked.

'Earlier.' Red answered. 'It says in the book on Stately Homes :
"Dates from 1480, a picturesque example of Tudor domestic
architecture. Owned by the Marquess of Northampton, D.S.O.
Wednesdays, Saturdays, and Bank Holidays, 10 to 12, 2 to 5." '

A plump and cheerful little woman took our money and asked
if we minded joining the other party, which turned out to be
two Amazons in whiskery tweeds. They ran a seaside resort in
Devon, they told us, and now that the season was over, they
were off on a busman's holiday. They didn't miss a thing : they
thumped the Silent Lady in the drawing-room, rapped the
panelling beside the staircase, assayed the amount of bullion in a
gold-embroidered tapestry, and tested the bounce in the mammoth Jacobean bed in which Henry VIII had once slept. All in
all, they saved us a lot of trouble.

At the top of the house lay the Council Chamber, a handsome
room in unstained oak, with bands of carved holly for trim.
Above it, reached by a twisty staircase hidden in a closet, was a
cubbyhole the guide called 'the priest's room'. The phrase was
apparently self-explanatory to the tweedy ladies, but I wanted
more. 'Why so hard to get to?' I asked. I was thinking, *The
chapel is three flights down, wouldn't you think they'd have
quartered the priest somewhere handier?*

'It was customary during the Reformation, madam. That

would be in 1530 or thereabouts,' the guide amplified. 'When England became Protestant, most of the nobles remained Catholic. But to do so openly wasn't—er—wise. This family, like so many, was Protestant downstairs and Catholic upstairs. This room is where they hid their priest.'

Meanwhile, George had been looking down into the garden. He turned to the guide and asked, 'Was there a moat?'

'Oh yes, sir, but it was filled in, sir, when the house was defortified after the Civil War. That was the price of its being returned to the owner.'

'The *English* Civil War,' Red hissed. 'In 1642, Puritan Parliament against Anglican King.'

The guide heard. 'This was a Royalist house, of course. Loyal to King Charles. Did you notice in the chapel that most of the glass is clear? The original stained glass was destroyed by the Roundheads.' Then, as we picked our way downstairs, 'If you have time before you leave, visit the parish church at the bottom of the drive. The tomb effigies there were mutilated at the same time. They were retrieved later from the moat.'

It was a pretty little church, the only one we saw in England with two aisles and a double-arched ceiling (like a pair of bread loaves). Originally one side had been a light colour and the other dark, to represent day and night, but all that remains of this whimsey is a fading sun and a waning moon preserved under glass.

We had intended to stay the night in Stratford, but it was so full of Ye Old Chintzy Tearoome and Ye Quaint Souvenir Shoppes that we kept right on going until we found a nice non-touristy two-star hotel in nearby Warwick. Then we returned to see *Hamlet* at the Shakespeare Memorial Theatre. The performance was full of heroic flourishes, sonorous soliloquies, and snippets of humour, and even George stayed wide awake through the bits that tend to drag. I can still see Ophelia, a blonde with a body as slight as a child's, twisting a lock of fair hair with eloquent, fluttering fingers. The memorable death that night was the death of her mind; it perished in weak spasms, like an abandoned kitten.

We awoke on Sunday to not-quite-fog, and to air so still the Avon was like grey glass. Framed by the muted reds and golds of turning trees, Warwick Castle rose wraithlike in the mist. Even the swans were still. We walked in silence across the bridge, feeling as if we should apologize to someone for our footfalls.

Suddenly George turned and looked back. 'Why does it look so familiar? We've never been here before.'

Red laughed. 'Disneyland, Pop.'

'*Disneyland?*' He looked again. 'Good Lord, you're right. It *does.*'

By the time we got to Kenilworth Castle, a lemon sun was weakly shining. Open to the elements, the Gothic-arched windows, in what must have been the great hall, made sharp silhouettes against the pale blue sky; all else was tumbling down in rosy ruins. We climbed a mound across the way so that we could look into what must have been elegant gardens when the Earl of Leicester threw his lavish parties there for Queen Elizabeth.

'Remember how Amy Robsart fell through the trap door?' I mused. 'They never proved he had her pushed, but I'll bet he did.'

'Who?' said Red. 'The Earl of Leicester? Over there?'

'The Earl of Leicester, but not over there. In a house near Oxford. In fact, she's buried in St Mary's. I've seen the marker.'

'*Who,* Mom?'

'Amy Robsart. The Earl of Leicester's wife. They said he got rid of her so he'd be free to marry Queen Elizabeth. Only she never asked him. That story was in *Kenilworth.* I remember weeping buckets. . . . You kids don't read Walter Scott any more in school, do you?'

As we clambered down from the mound, Red set the record straight. 'Sure we do. Some. I read *Lochinvar* in eighth grade. And I tried *Ivanhoe* just last year. But I quit after a couple of chapters. It had too many "forsooths" and thou hasts".'

'You could have finished it at the barbershop,' said George. 'They have it in their collection of comic books.'

'*George!*'

George grinned at Red. 'She always rises to the bait, doesn't she?'

Homeward bound in a lackadaisical Indian-summer mood, we rambled in loops and whorls through the lovely Cotswold countryside. Through Pillerton Hersey, Pillerton Priors, Fulready, Whatcote, and Whichford. Westering sun lay over the land like a benediction. Nothing moved. Even the bird song was hushed.

Beside the pretty, reed-edged Windrush River lies the tiny town of Minster Lovell. Of its ruined manor house, built in the fifteenth century, nothing remains complete, yet it's easy to people it with ghosts. A diamond-patterned, cobbled pathway leads to a squat-arched portico, beyond which lies the great hall, and one can pick out the shape of the rooms that once enclosed a tower from which I suppose the Barons Lovell watched for enemies. Rounding the base of that tower myself, I came face to face with a placid cow and yielded the field with a yelp. George said, 'Shoo, Boss,' and the cow ambled off. But the spell was broken: the Lovells returned to dust.

It was twilight now; the air was cold and wet, and streamers of mist were rising from the river. There would be hot soup at home, a cozy fire, and comfortable beds. Tomorrow was a school day. As the little pink house in Headington finally came into view, George said, 'Well, that was a very satisfying excursion into culture.' We all agreed, nodding at each other benignly.

Chapter 8

By November, Oxford was home. I would always be an alien, of course, but I was no longer a stranger.

I was wholly sold on the leisurely pace of English journalistic writing, which puts into the twelfth paragraph what American reporters are taught to put into the first. My eye slid without affront over such phrases as the 'the committee have . . .' or 'the government are . . .' and it was exceedingly restful to be free of Orphan Annie and Dick Tracy. To have ads on the front page of a newspaper now seemed right; in fact, I had become completely addicted to reading the daily appeals on behalf of the Society for the Assistance of Ladies in Reduced Circumstances, announcements of voice trials for church choir schools, offers to swap tickets for *My Fair Lady*, suggestions that household renovation problems be brought to the Woodworm and Dry Rot Centre, and the U.F.A.W.'s pleas that the reader buy a fur coat that had been humanely farmed rather than 'made of wild animals that died in long-drawn agony.'

On the domestic front I had washed my hands of the Rayburn as a cooker, a decision that had improved my disposition enormously. I had ceased longing for sturdy kitchen matches, paper towels, and the box-boys who sack your purchases in California supermarkets. I hardly saw the hogs' heads, neatly sawed in half, that were a staple item at the butcher shop. In making a telephone call from a public telephone I automatically pushed the A button to complete the connection, and I was making progress in crossing streets with English abandon (that is, whenever and wherever I felt like it)—a practice that had given all three of us regimented Californians a giddy sense of freedom. However, I was still looking in the wrong direction when I stepped into the street, and I couldn't seem to stop calling a block a block.

It wasn't difficult to switch, as a driver, to the left-hand side, but pedestrian habits must be much more deeply ingrained. All of us long continued to look left when we stepped off the curb; whereupon, with alarming frequency, we'd hear a squeal of brakes on the right. Even by the end of our Oxford year, when I *had* learned to look right, I never could quite resist the need to sneak a quick look left, just to make sure. I remember reading the memoirs of an English girl who had posed as French and had been a spy in Occupied France during World War II. The Gestapo finally nabbed her because she glanced involuntarily in the wrong direction while checking oncoming traffic.

As for blocks, the term isn't used, because few English cities are laid out on the grid system so common in America. You can see the difficulties one might run into: if four side roads enter a major street on its north side and none on its south side, how many blocks long is it? But this measure of distance is so deeply imbedded in American usage that I never quite broke myself of the habit of directing English acquaintances to our house by telling them that it was 'three blocks from the Headington traffic lights.' The English measure similar distances by time, as in: 'Jackstraws Lane? It's down the London Road a bit, and the house you're after will be just beyond the first turning. A ten-minute walk, I should say.' (With experience one learns to translate this into: 'Twenty minutes of hard walking will bring you close enough to ask for further directions while leaning against a wall and catching your breath.')

By November I knew at what point on the bus route the fare changed from fivepence to fivepence ha'penny; I had ceased to be startled by the fact that the street called North Parade was south of the one called South Parade; and I had learned that houses on different streets were not necessarily numbered after the same system. On some the even numbers were on one side of the street and the odd numbers on the opposite side, as in the United States; but every so often, having started with Number 1 on the south-east corner, I had found myself doggedly pursuing Number 20 up to the end of the street, across to the other side, and back down to the south-west corner, opposite Number 1.

Finally, I was making great strides with my English. Advanced level. I had mastered Basic English much earlier, and now knew as well as any native that electrical appliances have to be earthed, that a sponge is a cake, that a rag is a practical joke, and that a crocodile is a column of school children walking two-by-two. I had learned the hard way that I should not have asked for suspenders for George's pants) when what I really wanted was braces (for his trousers) unless I was prepared to take home garters (for my girdle). All *that* is elementary. I was now mastering the fine points.

I had very nearly figured out, for example, under what circumstances to add an extra 'do', 'have', or 'got'. (Ask an American, 'Are you going to town tomorrow?' and he responds, 'I might'. The Englishman says, 'I might do'.) I could say a proper 'thank you', which sounds something like 'nkew'. I was also making progress in the art of not saying anything, substituting a murmur in the throat for the expression of any emotion from acquiescence to indignation. And I knew what a hostess meant if she asked me whether I'd like to spend a penny. The euphemism arises out of the fact that it costs a penny to use a public rest room, only they're called public conveniences; and you've only yourself to blame if you ask for a bathroom when you don't want to have a bath. Incidentally, it's American to *take* one; and the only place in England where one bathes is at the seashore.

I was also learning—although I never mastered the art—to distinguish the delicate nuances of phrase and accent by which Englishmen gauge each other's class. It wasn't hard at either end of the scale, of course. The dropped or added 'h', the nasal vowels, and the affectionate diminutive are easily recognizable lower-class labels—just as the broad 'a', precise word choice, and careful articulation are marks of upper-class speech.

Our university acquaintances found it howlingly funny whenever George called me 'honey' (which he does habitually), because in so doing he was using lower-class idiom. And I must admit I was startled one day when a workman in a greasy trench coat and visored cap approached me on the street and asked, 'Can ye gi' me a penny for two ha'pennies, love?' This, and 'duck', have no more personal significance as forms of address than the upper-class 'sir' or 'madam'.

I was told that the conquering Normans, who spoke French, whereas the conquered Saxons spoke a Germanic tongue, set the precedent for an upper-class mode of speech. Now, nine hundred years later, the differences between upper and lower, or between regional and 'proper B.B.C.', or between Oxfordshire (county) and Oxford (university) are primary tools of social appraisal.

Whereas two Americans, falling into casual conversation on an airplane journey, have to *ask* each other about schools, clubs, favourite sports, and hobbies, in order to find out whether they might have mutual interests, two Englishmen in similar circumstances know everything they need to know about the other's background the minute they exchange their first words. (Assuming, of course, that they speak. However, if silence should continue long enough—say, from London to Istanbul—this in itself is a good indication that they are both Old Harrovians who should have spoken sooner because they would have had so much in common to talk about.)

It would be stupid to claim that there are no classes in the United States, but there is no widely recognized badge of caste comparable to that of English speech. Here—especially in the West—the educated or the well-born man speaks essentially like the shopkeeper or the telephone repairman, and the possession of a regional accent has no effect on social status or job opportunities. Personally, I like it that way. The class stratifications in England made me uncomfortable (a common American reaction there). But my encounter with our dustbin man at least demonstrated the *usefulness* of class-calibrated speech in working out social relationships. It came about this way:

Our dustbins (garbage cans) were emptied on Thursdays by a sparrow-like man with a leathery face, a spreading but virtually toothless smile, and a dialect so incomprehensible that it might as well have been Bantu. Like a code that needed solving, it intrigued me; and I took to popping out of the house whenever I heard the clatter of can covers. We got to be quite friendly, despite our almost total inability to communicate.

One day he arrived as I was taking a snapshot of Red in his school uniform. Observing the camera, he capered about so, pointing to himself, that I took a picture of him, too. The result was such a good likeness that I had an enlargement printed for him. But he did not react as I had thought he would. He stared at it disdainfully and tossed me such a skimpy 'thank you' that my feelings were hurt.

I related the incident to another professor's wife when she dropped in for a cup of coffee.

'I believe I know what the trouble was,' she said. 'The dustman would gratefully accept the picture as a gift from the lady of the house—and you *are* the lady of the house, of course. But he can't tell, by either your accent or your manner, what kind'—meaning class—'of person you are. So I expect he might have been afraid that you were about to propose *selling* him the picture. And if that should have been your intention, the less pleasure he showed the less likely you would have been to have set a high price.'

What my friend meant when she mentioned my manner was the free-'n'-easy assumption of equality with one's fellow-man that distinguishes Americans in England quite as much as their American accents. In the United States, although the upper classes and the lower classes are no likelier to dine at each other's homes than in England, there is less of a gulf between them in public life. They mingle with less self-consciousness because they have had more shared experiences. The P.T.A. and the Scouts are great levellers; everybody reads the same kind of middle-class newspaper; and anybody's child can go to college. As a result, we tend to think of each other as individuals, or as members of a certain economic or professional group, rather than as members of a certain social class.

This egalitarianism, and the 'Hi, Mac' form of address that grows out of it, both amuses and exasperates our foreign visitors. 'It's not that I want the lad at the petrol pumps to address me with cap in hand,' complained one of our distinguished English visitors, justly proud of his professorship, his D.Phil., and his O.B.E. 'But I must admit I cringe when he bellows out, "Harya today, Doc? Fillerup?" ' (I have been thinking about him afresh just now: as I typed this paragraph, a United Parcel delivery-man brought a package—and lingered long enough to say, 'Your new landscaping looks swell. I've been meaning to tell you.')

Except for noticeable deviants from the norm of dress and manner—slouching boys with duck-tail haircuts, for example—a certain kind of behaviour is not, in the United States, equated with a certain social class. In England, alas for me, it *is*. I remember with shame the day I jollied the bus conductor into allowing my unauthorized presence aboard his big red juggernaut.

From the beginning of our stay in Oxford I had been annoyed by the location of the railroad bus stop. It was necessary to disembark on the far side of a busy and sometimes treacherous street, then pick your way across as best you could. While you were dodging traffic, the bus was making a U-turn across the same street. Then it paused at the curb on the station side before it began its return trip to the city centre.

As the bus approached the station stop on the particular day I am remembering, I suddenly thought, *Why shouldn't I make the U-turn with the bus?* I was the only passenger aboard, and decided to chance it. So I announced to the bus conductor that I'd ride across the street.

'Not allowed, ma'am,' he said.

'Oh, come on,' I wheedled, giving him the kind of a smile that used to produce bacon from under the counter during the war. 'You're going over there anyway. Be a sport.' I spoke with the same bantering cajolery I expend on parking-lot attendants, at home, when I'd like them to call my hour and five minutes of parking time an even hour. Sometimes I make it ('For a gorgeous doll like you?'—I'm definitely a matron—'Sure!'), and sometimes I don't ('Lady, with a swanky car like yours'—it's a '51 Plymouth—'you can spare the dough.') No hard feelings, either way.

But the English bus conductor didn't respond in kind, as his American counterpart would have done; he just turned away and signalled the driver to start. Feeling half elated and half let down, I sat silent while the bus swung into the street and completed its turn; then overcompensated by uttering a too effusive 'thank you' as I rose from my seat to descend.

The bus conductor came vigorously to life. Flashing a big gold grin, he responded, 'Me pleasure, duck!' And squeezed me around my waist as he helped me down.

I stamped up to the station, embarrassed, ashamed, and outraged. I was still sizzling when I reported the incident to George that evening. 'That wouldn't have happened at home. Now, *would* it? Of course not! An American bus driver wouldn't get fresh just because I kidded him along. Now, *would* he?'

George laughed until he cried—which made me even angrier, and more ashamed. After that I minded my manners.

One of the complaints that some foreign exchange students express, after spending a year in the United States, is that visitors here don't meet a broad enough sample of Americans. That's true. Foreign students tend to be most welcome in academic and upper-middle-class circles. Joe Doakes, who runs the bottle-capping machine at the soft-drink plant, is usually too shy or too uninterested in other cultures to venture far from his TV set or expand his world much beyond the familiar faces he knows at the plant, the union hall, the bowling alley, or his lodge.

So it was with us at Oxford. We were immobilized in the academic group—not that we struggled any, for they were charming, witty friendly people—and our knowledge of 'the working classes' came from casual encounters in stores, hotels, and on trains. We never got to know our gardener at all; he came and went as if he'd been ectoplasm. I never met any of Mrs Blount's family, although I knew a lot about them; or saw her home. We didn't patronize the pub across the street, because it was not natural for us to do so. Our social needs had many other outlets, and the regular patrons would have rightly suspected that we were there merely to observe the quaint customs of the natives.

Within the university circle it was, of course, the wives I came to know. They were upper-class by birth or by reason of education, and what they lacked in gusto they made up for in grace. Their self-control was a delight to watch and a model to copy. Once I was a tea guest when the man of the house was fifteen minutes late. The hostess was in a dreadful spot: should she keep me waiting, a crime against convention, or proceed without the host? She waited, and when her husband came strolling in—without apologies—she said, without any show of anger, 'Alfred, it was naughty of you to have been so late today.' In similar circumstances I couldn't have resisted the urge to have shot him just *one* you-heel-you glance.

Oxford wives work hard. And they don't complain. They don't participate in community welfare activities to the extent that American women of the same class do, but I dare say *we* wouldn't have enough energy to join political action groups, discuss the Great Books, attend School Board meetings, ring doorbells for the Cancer Fund, and pour orange juice at the Bloodmobile, if we had to spend as much time in obsolete kitchens as our English counterparts do.

One activity they are spared is the car pool. Two-car families are rare in England, and there are plenty of no-car families still, so Sonny gets where he has to go by bus, bike, or shanks' mare.

Unfortunately Mum does too. She is usually seen trudging along
the streets with a canvas satchel in one hand a string bag in the
other, both bulging with the day's food purchases. Or she hops
on her bike and wheels down to Sainsbury's at the crack of dawn
—meaning 8.45 a.m., the English being late risers—hoping that
she'll be first in the queue for that day's special on cheese. On her
way home she stops at the launderette to see if the notice she
posted in search of domestic help is still on view; she's had no
replies. It's there, all right, and so are a dozen other pleas just
like it, all growing dusty and frayed. She stops next at the ironmonger's to order paraffin for her stoves, making a mental note
at the same time to trim the wick on the one in the dining-room;
it's gone a bit smoky. Then she matches a bit of yarn at the
draper's, picks up a skirt and a suit at the dry cleaner's, and
arrives home in a sprint because it has started to rain and there
is laundry on the lines out back.

More and more English women are acquiring labour-saving
appliances, but the heart of the housework problem is that their
houses are badly engineered, especially the numerous surviving
Victorian ones with the scullery in the basement, the dining-
room on the floor above, the drawing-room above that, and the
bedrooms still higher. If there's anything to be said in praise of
retribution it can surely be said that today's English wife under-
stands the lot of her grandmother's Irish servant girls much
better than grandmother did.

The really rich still have servants, of course, just as they do in
the United States. And some of the great houses are still run with
as much style as in the old days. The experience of one American
we know attests to *that*. He was weekending at the home of a
British peer, and on retiring was detained by the butler.

'Would you care for morning tea, sir?' the butler asked.

'Why, yes, that would be very nice,' the American responded
as he started up the stairs.

'Pardon, sir. Would you prefer India, Ceylon, or China?'

'India, I guess,' and the American took another upward step.

'Milk or lemon, sir?'

'Oh. Milk, please.' Assuming that the conversation had ter-
minated, the American turned away and began to climb briskly.

But from below came a final question. 'Er, one more thing, sir.
Alderney, Jersey, or Friesian?'

This kind of service will undoubtedly endure, on both sides of the Atlantic, within the homes of that tiny fraction of the population that has the ability to obtain it and the capacity to appreciate it. What has changed in the United States and is changing in England is the availability of servants to the upper-middle and professional classes. Dons' wives in Oxford two generations ago would have had a cook or a maid; today they're lucky to have a 'daily'. They are forced, therefore, to work as hard as the servants their predecessors once employed—just to keep their families clean and fed.

But that's not the whole of their problem. They are forced to observe, or are clinging to, niceties of etiquette that further burden them. I put away my damask tablecloths years ago, and so did most American housewives, because we haven't time to wash and iron them and still be Den Mothers. We've shifted— not without some feeling of guilt, to be sure—to stainless-steel flatware and to paper napkins, to drip-dry clothes and to one-bowl cake mixes. But Englishwomen haven't made these compromises yet—partly because they can't afford the extra cost of preprocessed food or commercial laundry charges, but also because they are still trying to do things *nicely*. In consequence they are still polishing heirloom silver, ironing sheets and shirts, dusting Dresden bric-a-brac, and cooking at least four meals a day.

What I came to call the English non-dinner hour plagued us from our first week in Oxford, and was one of the few situations to which I never grew reconciled. In part this was due to my refusal to spend as much time in the kitchen as Englishwomen do, and in part because it has been our long-time family custom to share the news of our separate activities at a communal—and early—dinner. The elimination from American schedules of afternoon tea, which in England is more than a snack but less than a meal, keeps us all more or less on the same eating timetable. But in England, after 4 p.m., everything falls apart.

If father is dining out that night, mother may turn tea into supper for herself and the children at five. The same thing may happen if both parents are going to the theatre, with curtain time at seven, except that they'll be hungry again at ten, so Mum will fix a light supper after the performance. If the household's regular dinner hour is at eight, and nobody's going anywhere, and the children are so starved when they come home from school that an early meal is indicated, Mum feeds them at five-thirty and herself and father at eight. Unless, of course, father has to go to a meeting at eight, in which case she prepares a light tea at four and they all eat dinner at seven.

English husbands are not indifferent to the plight of their wives. The Saturday shopping crowds are full of fathers trailing children after them like the tail on a kite, and many of them routinely lend a hand with the washing up after dinner. But woman's work is still exclusively woman's work to a much greater extent than in the United States. One senses a kind of separateness, of husbands and wives keeping segments of their lives closed from each other—not in a spirit of concealment, but simply because men and women are assumed to have different interests and non-overlapping responsibilities.

Husbands and wives go about together socially less than we do in America. Each is likely to have separate clubs. Although women are not excluded at the pub across the street from our house in Headington, the majority of patrons were men. The wives, presumably, had had their social outing during the day. And even when the sexes are together, there is far less fuss about Fair Guinevere than in the United States. American men are said to spoil their women. I guess they do; it's a hangover from the frontier, where there were never enough women to go around. In England hotel waiters are the only men who hold chairs for ladies as they seat themselves at the dining table. Englishwomen get along without much show of gallantry and seem resigned to a lower status in society than their militant American sisters will accept. There is usually a differential between men's and women's salaries, even if they are doing the same work, and fewer educational opportunities exist for women. Against which can be set the emotional security that comes from knowing who you are and what is expected of you: the English are less confused than Americans about the rôles to assign, in the family and in society, to men and women. In England the diapers—no, the nappies—are still changed by women.

Now, anything that's generally true of England is exaggerated in Oxford.

Shortly after our arrival there, and before I realized that I was going to be spending so much of my time with women, I had been invited to dinner by a don's wife. She is a talented sculptress, and after dinner she showed her guests around her studio. One piece particularly caught my eye. It was some ten inches high and depicted two figures. The dominant one was a lion of a man in academic regalia, his gown falling in massive folds from his shoulders to his firmly planted feet. Head back, chin up, paunch rounding gently forward, this was a man with the universe in the palm of his hand. He was unmistakably an Oxford don. A step behind him stood a dowdy little woman. There was a shapeless hat on her meekly bowed head, a shapeless jacket drooping from her slightly stooped shoulders, the hint of a wrinkle in her stockings. Equally unmistakably, she was the don's wife. The title of the figurine was, *It's a Man's World*.

It's a man's world at Oxford because, as Roger Mackenzie had explained, so many of the colleges have an ecclesiastical—even a monastic—background, and ritual observances have a way of persisting at the university long after the social structure they once reflected has passed away. The decision, at the end of the nineteenth century, that dons might marry was forced on a reluctant university by the obvious fact that many of them were raising families in North Oxford houses just beyond the university's jurisdiction.

So, too, the medieval position of women remains in more than memory. During Janet Lindvall's visit George and I had taken her to Evensong at Christ Church College chapel. When we entered the nave, by the transept, which separates the altar and the choir from the lower pews and in the middle of which stands the Bible on its goldern lectern, the verger had indicated that we were to go left, into the lower pews. But he had detained George long enough to say that *he* might go right, if he cared to, closer to the altar. It seems that in Christ Church chapel women may not sit above the Bible.

It's been only forty years since women have been admitted to the university. Some of the old-timers still consider it a regrettable decision. There is a rule that a don need not deliver scheduled lecture if fewer than two people are present; and one old misogynist, a few years back, on finding a male and a female undergraduate awaiting him, addressed the gentleman thus: 'Sir, since you are the only person present, I shall not lecture today.'

The girl undergraduates—they are never called 'coeds', because no undergraduate college is coeducational—are hedged in by more restrictions than the men, may still not join certain university clubs, have a stricter code of behaviour. But they have come a long way from that period when, the story goes, a girl was sent down from her Oxford college because she had spoken to a male cousin in the street. ('It is not so much the grave immorality of your conduct I deplore,' her Principal had said. 'It is the terrible bad taste.')

Little by little the university is letting the girls move into the twentieth century. Or perhaps it would be more accurate to say that the last two reforms have been achieved by feminine vanity, a potent weapon even at Oxford, and one that the dons have been unable to combat. They have long ceased enforcement of the no-lipstick rule during examinations; and theirs was, at best, a pyrrhic victory on the issue of whether the girls might wear nylon hose with the sober black and white garb prescribed for university ceremonials. The assumption of the 1920s was that the girl's black stockings would be opaque, but modern technology changed all that. The girls'—er—limbs became so noticeable, as nylons got more sheer, that a special university committee was convened a few years ago to consider the problem. After a bit of wrangling, it was decided that female undergraduates might continue to wear nylons *only if they had a seam up the back*. What this has accomplished, as far as I could see, is to trace even better the curve of a comely calf. Furthermore, some of the girls wear their black skirts very short and full, and elongate their ribbons ties so they reach below the waist—a *très chic* costume, especially in conjunction with those filmy nylons. Such outfits meet all the statutory requirements, yet somehow the total effect isn't at all what I think the dons had in mind when they drew up the rules.

Members of the men's and women's colleges meet at lectures, share a certain amount of club life, and presumably sometimes date each other. But the impression a visitor gets watching clusters of undergraduates come and go across town, is that men and women are far more segregated than at an American university—and need each other less. One senses the same apartness in them that is characteristic of their elders. They seem to be easier in the company of their own sex. Maybe the sex-segregated lower schools are to blame; with very few exceptions the grammar and public schools are not coeducational. There is no doubt that

America's high marriage rate among teen-agers is encouraged by proximity. But perhaps the English system goes too far to the other extreme, diverting youthful passions to the playing fields so successfully that too little ardour remains for people. Or perhaps the English coolness is just on the surface, a hangover of Victorian propriety, for they certainly haven't always been that way. The Elizabethans greeted strangers with a kiss. Today it's all you can do to get them to shake hands.

Which brings to mind George Mikes's unsurpassed summary of English domestic relations. A Hungarian by birth and a Briton by naturalization, he says, 'Continental people have sex life. The English have hot-water bottles.'

Chapter 9

I HAVE DONE my husband an injustice. I've given the impression that he's an average American husband and father, cooler-tempered than some, warmer-hearted than others, an ex-Nebraska farm boy who has never outgrown an addiction to puns and who in Britain acquired an addiction to prehistoric relics. All that is true. But the most important fact about George is that he's a scientist. I think he would have come home if both the laboratory and the house had caught fire at the same time, but I'm glad he never had to make such an agonizing choice.

Scientists are not necessarily odd. But they *are* curious, and when a good one tackles a problem whose solution, he feels intuitively, is hovering somewhere just over his shoulder, he is likely to spend a good deal of time on it. That's what George had done. His specialty is genetics: the science of heredity. It is a young science, dating from the rediscovery, in 1900, of Mendel's classic paper on his experiments with peas, but George's particular biochemical brand of genetics is much younger, dating only from the 1920s. Earlier geneticists had concentrated mostly on the mechanics of inheritance. (Is eye colour controlled by one gene or several? How are genes arranged in the chromosomes?) George and scientists like him grew interested in the functioning and structure of the genes themselves. It seemed likely that they were not merely passive carriers of hereditary characteristics but active directors of chemical processes, also.

So George teamed up with a chemist friend, E. R. Tatum, and the two of them did an experiment to find out. They irradiated millions of plants of *Neurospora crassa*, a red mould that grows on bread, thus causing mutations (changes) in some of the genes. If genes control chemical processes—metabolism is a basic one—some of the next generation of *Neurospora* plants should fail to function properly, Beadle and Tatum figured.

And that (although I'm oversimplifying) is how it worked out. Eventually they found a mould that functioned just like its parent mould except that it could not make Vitamin B₁, *and the reason was one altered gene.* Later they found dozens of other examples that could mean only one thing: that genes not only carry the recipe for the man who is to grow out of a fertilized egg cell, but they also direct his chemistry of growth, development, and functioning.

This was a great discovery, and is the reason my husband is well enough known in science to have been invited to Oxford. It is also the reason for his being awarded, in December of that year, the Nobel Prize given annually to a scientist who has done notable work in the field of physiology or medicine. He shared the honour with his co-worker, Ed Tatum, and with Joshua Lederberg, a younger scientist who, in applying their findings to bacteria, had made some great discoveries of his own.

A Nobel Prize is the top accolade a scientist can receive. Getting it would be unalloyed joy if it came like a bolt from the blue, but George had almost a week of cliff-hanging before the official announcement was made. The news leaked to newspaper reporters in Stockholm, they alerted the international wire services, and for a long seven days a non-stop press conference went on in the homes and labs of that year's Nobel laureates. Reporters and photographers hounded Tatum in New York and Lederberg in Wisconsin and Beadle in England.

'How do you feel about this great honour?' they asked. 'What will you do with all that money?' The first question has only one answer—'Fine!'—and the second is none of their business; besides, how do you answer such questions when you don't know for sure that you've actually won the prize? On a number of occasions the rumoured recipients have in fact been passed over, and George was determined not to assume that he had been awarded the prize until he had an official notification from Stockholm in hand. The waiting was hard; on the day before the official announcement was due, he came home and said, with a rueful smile, 'Well, I *am* in a stew. After I finished my lecture today, I discovered I'd given it backward.'

But the rumours were based on truth, and, with confirmation, the atmosphere changed to jubilee. George could not have taken two steps on the Caltech campus without having his hand shaken or his back slapped; but this was England. To spare him the embarrassment of public attention, none of his colleagues at the lab or at the college mentioned his award in company. Those who happened to run into him when he was alone cleared their throats diffidently, essayed a mild handshake, and murmured, 'Splendid news about your—er—honour'; or simply, 'Good show!' It would have been a lonely time for him if breezy American greetings hadn't come pouring in by cable, sea, and air.

'After all the publicity over the Pasternak affair,' wrote a friend at Yale, 'I have taken a poll. The general feeling here is that you ought to accept it; to hell with trying to keep up with the Russians.'

With typical irreverence a group of graduate students in the Caltech biology division wired: TREMENDOUSLY PLEASED AND PROUD. COME HOME. BRING MONEY. Among the list of signatories one name—no odder than any of the others, from Western Union's viewpoint—appeared, but upon seeing it George laughed until he had to wipe away the tears. This 'signatory' was N. Crassa: his old friend, *Neurospora crassa*, the red bread mould.

His mirth diminished, however, and was replaced by a bulldog tenacity when he received a two-page cable in code. He recognized it immediately as the work of a colleague at Caltech, because it was based on the four units of nucleic acid that make up the genes. (It is the specific sequence of these units that spells out the 'message' of the gene.) George had to do a preliminary translation from chemical biology into the English alphabet before he could even start to decode the message, and he must have put in forty frustrating hours on it. Solved at last, it read: 'Break this code or give back Nobel Prize.' George said that it was a mighty close call.

The messages piled up on the desk and overflowed to the dining-room table. The motorcycle-mounted delivery boys, who at first had thrust each cablegram at me as breathlessly as if they were bringing serum to a dying child, now lounged in the doorway with a sheaf of envelopes and a bored ' 'Ere's another lot of 'em, ma'am.'

But Mrs Blount remained enormously impressed. One day George found her reverently dusting the pile. 'These are all cables, Mr Beadle?' she inquired. He assented, and then she said, 'Just think of that! To have come all that way under the ocean. It's a miracle, like!'

To this day I tend to think of the Atlantic Cable as Mrs Blount did. There's something very satisfying in the mental picture of a gigantic pneumatic tube on the ocean floor, with slips of paper scurrying back and forth like change and sales receipts in a department store.

There were letters and conferences originating in England, too. Sir Hans Krebs, professor of biochemistry at Oxford and a Nobel laureate in 1953, invited us over for tea and briefed us on what the actual presentation ceremony in Stockholm would be like. Willis Lamb, an American who is now Oxford's professor of physics and who won his Nobel Prize in 1955, warned us to take an extra set of studs and plenty of safety pins. He broke the only collar button he had with him just before the very formal awards ceremony got under way. Consequently his recollection of the ceremony is a little fuzzy; he was afraid to turn his head and almost afraid to breathe, for fear the smallish safety pin that held his collar and his shirt together would suddenly yield to the strain.

My own dress presented no problem, and we solved George's special wardrobe requirements by renting a full-dress suit with three complete sets of accessories. But what of Red? Letters flew back and forth between me and Mrs Sanger (whose husband, a Cambridge professor, had won the chemistry prize that year for his discovery of the molecular structure of insulin) as to what our schoolboy sons should wear. Neither of us liked the idea of putting fifteen-year-olds into white ties and tails, so we decided on dinner jackets for them. I forthwith rented a tuxedo for Red. I can still hear his pleased and startled 'We-e-ll!' as he glimpsed in the pier glass the suave man-about-town he had suddenly become.

In memory, the Nobel festivities are still like a dream in Technicolour. Commoners do not dine with kings, except in fairy tales, yet there we were, on December 10th in Stockholm's Concert Hall, its gold mosaic walls ablaze with the light reflected from thousands of candles—guests at the table of a reigning monarch. And the next evening we dined at the Palace, its drawing-room, that cold midwinter night, was a spring bower of white lilacs and primroses.

King Gustav is a tall, kindly man, surprisingly vigorous for his years. He made conversation easy. Queen Louise, English born, has a great simplicity and gentleness of manner. The young princesses, Margaretha, Birgitta and Desirée, looked exactly as princesses in a fairy tale *should* look. All the ladies of the royal family wore pale-coloured ball gowns, with broad Swedish blue sashes across the bodices, and tiaras and beautiful jewellery.

In addition to the two major banquets, there were cocktail parties, receptions and dinners: a lavish week-long outpouring of hospitality. The Russians were the focus of special interest everywhere because that was the year in which the poet Boris Pasternak had 'not wished to accept' his prize, although three Russian physicists had claimed their rewards. The Swedish press dogged them; guests at various parties eyed them covertly, and the Russian ambassador hovered over them like a nervous mother hen.

We made the acquaintance of schnapps and smoked reindeer, and learned the etiquette of *sköl*. The Swedes are enthusiastic drinkers, speechmakers, and handshakers. They made us realize how much we had missed in England the heartiness and lack of constraint in social relationships to which we had been accustomed in the United States. Or maybe, our sudden homesickness was just a yearning for the simple and uncomplicated life we led in California. As natives of a country that pays more attention to its movie stars than to its academicians, we were uneasy in the rôle of celebrities. One night George said, with great wistfulness, 'Honey, I wish I were home making compost.'

The royal coach turned into a pumpkin soon enough. On December 15th London was fogbound and our returning plane was diverted to Manchester. From there a long, slow crawl—three hours longer than the flight from Sweden—took us to Oxford. We arrived home at 3 a.m., to clammy sheets and a cold Rayburn.

The next morning, when we all felt better, George said to me, 'Wow! Another week like that one and I'd have never gotten you into the kitchen again.'

George came upon me, a week later, morosely wrapping up a book I'd bought for Red for Christmas. The paper was a thin tissue of poor quality, and the only ribbon I'd been able to find in Headington was a sleazy quarter-inch rayon.

'It just won't make a proper bow,' I complained.

'Don't take it so hard,' George said.

'And the stores don't have any gift boxes.'

'Gad, that's awful.'

'Well, you don't have to be sarcastic about it. Sure, it's trivial, but Christmas trimmings mean a lot to me.'

'I'm sorry, honey,' he began.

'Don't apologize! and don't sympathize!' I snapped. Then, contrite, 'George, I'm sorry. I'm *homesick.*' I hid Red's book among the linens; happily *that* closet was free of mildew. 'Maybe it's the dismal weather. Wouldn't it be nice to sit in hot California sun for just an hour?'

'Have an orange,' he said. (We'd been sent a whopping big box of Arizona citrus fruit; you'd have thought, from the way we dug in, that we all had scurvy.)

As I ate my half, I expressed another regret. 'It was stupid to have mailed our gifts to the folks at home before we went to Sweden. There were so many wonderful things I could have bought in Stockholm, light enough to have gone by air mail.'

'Now, honey. What you did send was very nice. You said so yourself. Especially the toys.' He looked at me shyly, and I made a face at him, and then we both laughed. My blue mood began to lift.

The day I bought the toys had started like this:

'How come you're all dressed up?' Red had asked at breakfast.

'And what's the rush?' George had added.

'Because,' I had answered them both, scooping up their egg plates and plunging them into the dishpan while their forks were still in mid-air, 'I have to go Christmas shopping in London. I hate to go shopping in London. For that matter, I hate to go to London.'

They knew I did. It was necessary to take two buses to get from Headington to the Oxford railroad station, then ride for an hour and a half in a musty railroad carriage. In the city I would put in five hours beating my way from one unfamiliar store to another, being jostled on the sidewalks, and getting lost on the Underground. Finally, the whole train-bus sequence would have to be repeated, at the height of the rush hour, with queues a block long, and by then it would be raining.

'But why London?' George had asked. 'Why don't you get what you want in Oxford?'

'Because I can't, that's why. The gifts for the children back home, anyway. The least we can do, it seems to *me*, is to send them typically English toys. And all I've seen in Oxford are Roy Rogers guns and Wells Fargo stagecoaches. Imagine that! In *England!*'

George, who knows as well as any husband that a wifely tempest based on a point of trifling importance is the kind most likely to annihilate the innocent bystander, had made some non-committal but sympathetic noises. Then he had said, 'Tell you what. I'll meet the train. Save you the bus ride home.'

This had been an incredibly generous offer on his part, for it meant that he would twice have to drive through the traffic tangle at the Carfax—and at its peak of ferocity. For a moment I had been tempted to be a martyr and refuse, but I had finally thanked him and said that I'd appreciate his meeting me.

Which he had done, and I *was* grateful, for I'd made the train with only seconds to spare, and there were six people in all the second-class compartments already. Even though each compartment is supposed to hold eight, passengers who claim the seventh and eighth places are always treated to a battery of drop-dead looks from those who have to make room for them, and that's what had happened to me. Besides, the racks were full of the other passengers' boxes, brief cases, suitcases, shopping bags, Thermos kits, overcoats, raincoats, bowlers, bundles, and books, so I'd had to hold mine on my lap the whole two hours en route. Not that the trip should have taken so long, but at Didcot the train had just sat in the dark and panted for thirty minutes.

When I'd finally squeezed my way past the gate guard at Oxford, splashed through the puddles, found the shelter of the car, and dumped the packages on the back seat, George had said cheerily, 'Well, it looks like you had luck with your shopping.'

'Yes.'

Halfway up Headington hill he had tried again. 'Pleased with what you got?'

'I guess so.' I was beginning to relax. 'Yes, I am. The toys especially. The nieces and nephews will love them.'

'Good.' Now that he could tell that I was calming down, George said what he had wanted to say that morning. 'Honey, I wish you wouldn't knock yourself out like this. It wouldn't have mattered whether they were "typically English" toys or not.'

'As a matter of fact, they're not.' And then I had giggled.

'Even in London I couldn't find one darned English-made toy that I couldn't have duplicated in America. The ones I got were all imported from *Germany*.'

England doesn't make as much of a fuss about Christmas as the United States does. All in all, it was rather pleasant not to have one's sense of anticipation whipped into a frenzy. Father Christmas was allowed to stay at the North Pole instead of being forced to serve time on red plush thrones in department-store Toylands. There were no Christmas trees sprayed pink or blue, and no reindeers and sleighs poised, floodlit, on roof tops. There weren't even any holly wreaths—to speak of—on the doors. 'An American custom, that,' the nurseryman told me when I bought our three-foot Christmas tree. 'But it's beginning to catch on here, too.'

Even before we'd gone to Stockholm, we'd begun to get Christmas cards from home. These were from well-organized friends who had bought their cards in August, affixed the stamps in October, and whipped them off the minute the 'Post Early' placards had gone up at the post office. The bulk came later, of course, splashy with air-mail stamps, our address so swiftly scrawled it was barely legible. What a good many of these cards had in common was that they had been chosen especially for us, and featured Victorian carollers warbling under gaslit street lights, boars' heads being borne into medieval halls, or stage-coaches pulling up on snowy roads at English inn doors. A customary postscript said something to the effect that the sender was terribly envious to think of us celebrating Christmas amid traditional scenes of this sort.

Snow? We had a dusting. Oxford rarely has snow before Christmas, and not much after. Carollers? Oh yes. We had *them* —by the dozens. They were mostly urchins. They came in groups of two or three, their grubby fingers clutching worn hymnals and their faces blue with cold. Invited inside, they sang a carol or two in thin little voices, eyes fixed on the ceiling and socks falling down, pocketed a coin apiece, and departed blushing. These onslaughts by the young resembled nothing so much as the visits of Halloween trick-or-treatsters at home, and the novelty of hearing 'Adeste Fideles' as a soprano duet finally wore off. One evening, when George answered the doorbell, I heard him say, 'As it happens, we're busy right now. But here's a shilling. Why don't you go sing a carol for someone else?'

Red got invited to a spate of dancing parties—the only time during our stay that he had any social contact with girls. The parties themselves were more like dancing classes than the parties he goes to at home, but in one respect they were identical. Whenever, at a December sherry party, I happened to mention that we had a fifteen-year-old son, my companion would often become extremely cordial, details of Red's dossier would be delicately extracted, and the next mail would bring him an invitation to a dance. Extra men are apparently as scarce in England, and as prized, as in the United States.

'What'll I wear, Mom?' he asked when he was getting ready to dress for the first party.

'Your grey flannel suit and a sober tie,' I replied. I'd been caught out on many a detail of English etiquette, but this time I knew that I was on firm ground. English teen-agers are much less precocious socially than their American cousins. They're allowed far less freedom, remain subordinate to the adults in the family much longer, begin to date much later. Consequently I was sure that their party clothes would compare to those an American twelve-year-old would wear to a wedding.

When Red returned from the party that night, and when in the course of the post-mortem I got around to the who-wore-what, he said, 'Guess how many grey flannel suits there were? Two. The other guys wore tuxes.'

'Good gracious! What did the girls wear?'

'The girls? I didn't notice. Dresses, I guess.'

(Men! I checked this detail at a subsequent party. The girls weren't precisely in strapless tulle, but they weren't wearing prim little navy velveteens with lace collars, either.)

The next morning at breakfast Red remembered an unreported tidbit. 'You know how cars drive on the left here?'

'Yes?'

'Feet do too. At home the man leads off on the right foot. Here he leads off on the left. I sure stepped on a lot of toes last night.'

But he received other invitations and kept on going—in his grey flannel suit. Nobody cared. Bless the English.

The weather, which hadn't been really bad, turned awful just before Christmas. Coincidentally my mother arrived for a visit.

She shivered and shook, but her upper lip is as stiff as any Briton's, and soon the house began to show signs of her presence. The tub in which I'd set our little Christmas tree acquired a shiny skirt of aluminium foil. The few plants in the solarium that had survived my haphazard care began to look as if somebody loved them, and our silver gleamed.

It is from my mother that I have acquired my sentimental attachment to traditions, whether within the family or on a broader scale, hence I was particularly pleased that she was with us on Christmas Eve at Magdalen College. There, for an enchanted four hours, Merrie Olde England came to life.

The great hall was garlanded with evergreens. Their pungent fragrance, released by the warmth of candles massed on ledges around the room, mingled with aroma of mince and sausage pies and the tantalizing spicy smell of mulled wine. William of Waynflete—generally referred to as The Founder—looked down upon us from the walls, along with other venerable churchmen, nobles, and Old Members. Perhaps their smiling ghosts were at our elbows as we filled the cup, drained the barrels, trilled the ancient Christmas carols. There was certainly *some* presence in the room that was not of this century. The choirboys sang the old, old carols—'Lullay my liking', 'The Holly and the Ivy', 'Ding dong merrily'—as well as a Bach oratorio, their voices soaring sweet and high above a mellow bass recorder. Just before midnight we all launched into 'Adeste Fideles'. Warmed by wine and good fellowship, our voices beat against the rafters on the final *'Venite adore-ay-mu-us Do-o-minum.'* And then everyone fell silent. A prickle of anticipation coursed through the hall. Finally, far and away, in silver notes, the college clock chimed twelve. *'Gloria in excelsis Deo!'* the choir exulted. A loving cup, garlanded with ribbons, made the rounds. And then the tower bells began to peal . . .

Change-ringing is a uniquely English art. It combines four or more bells of different pitch—Magdalen has ten—each of which is rung in a different pattern. The rhythms overlap, blending into a rolling, tumbling medley of sound that makes the heart lift and the spine tingle any time you hear it. But on that particular Christmas Day in the morning, as we left the college, the clangor of bells overwhelmed and enveloped us. They beat us to earth.

They tossed us heavenward. Even the cold stars seemed to shimmer in the midnight sky, and the rapture was almost imposssible to bear.

After that anything would have been an anticlimax. Yet our own family Christmas celebration was warm and jolly, the roast chicken an unqualified success, and we spent a cozy afternoon chatting about Christmases past and Christmases yet to come. In the evening we witnessed another traditional Oxford celebration of the season: the Singing of the Boar's Head Carol at Queen's College.

Once upon a long time ago the Fellows of Queen's *did* assemble on Christmas night to eat a boar's head decked with flags and gilded holly, and it is the bringing to table of this delicacy that is still commemorated. But only a handful of dutiful Fellows gather at High Table now, and only for the ten minutes it takes the procession to advance through the hall—first the cantor, then the choirboys, finally the cooks holding the boar's head aloft on a heavy silver platter. It was a pretty parade, but somehow it was as two-dimensional in effect as the same scene on one of those Christmas cards we'd received from home. Perhaps making a fuss over a boar's head that nobody was going to eat gave the ceremony its essential hollowness.

On the day after Christmas, Boxing Day, England collapses. Nothing runs, no newspapers are published, and people either slump deep in their armchairs at home and look at the telly, or go to visit friends and drink mulled wine. The regulars at the pub across the street had a riotous party, from which they exited flushed and merry, wearing paper caps and tooting toy horns and revving up a storm on their motorcycles before they went swooshing off into the night.

The Darlingtons had asked us to attend a Christmas pantomime with them. 'They're as traditional as plum pudding,' Gwendolen had said. 'Let's all see *Cinderella*. The children too, of course.'

Mother and I were delighted. George and Red were wary. Cinderella is a saccharine tale to start with, and to see it interpreted without dialogue (that's why, by definition, a pantomime is; or so we thought) sounded much too hearts-and-flowery to my menfolk. But affection for the Darlingtons tipped the scales, and we accepted.

Well!

The performance started pretty much as we had expected, with the fluffy little blonde who played Cinderella scouring the pots and pans in the castle kitchen. Then the scene moved to a garden, where we met Prince Charming. At this point I did a double take: it was obvious, as His Highness came mincing across a bridge, that he was a female. Rather gorgeously so, too: I've never seen longer, shapelier, or better displayed legs. While he—she?—was warbling a love song to Cinderella, I shot a glance at Mother. Her lips had drawn into a disapproving line. I felt squirmy myself. This was all very—er—*irregular*.

I whispered to Gwendolen, 'Isn't it a little odd to cast a woman in that rôle?'

She whispered back, 'Not at all. The Principal Boy is always a woman. With good legs. It's traditional.'

The real love interest, it turned out, was supplied by a male character called Buttons—a simple villager, he, who kept trying to win Cinderella right up to the final scene with the slipper. By that time, however, the actual sex of Prince Charming was immaterial, for we had gasped with laughter through a dozen scenes dominated by the Ugly Sisters—who were *men* ('it's traditional')—and clowns, besides. In addition to their slapstick, in the grand tradition of the Keystone Kops, we had endured some off-colour jokes, had politely applauded a ballet sequence featuring a group of earnest but muscle-bound maidens, and had been truly charmed by some well-drilled child dancers called Vera Legge's Moonbeam Babes. They did a precision drill with hula hoops, a Charleston that was the cat's meow, and—well, somehow, we lost track of Cinderella.

On leaving the theatre we ran into the Morrises, also with their children in tow. They asked how we'd liked our first exposure to an English pantomime.

George was still wiping his eyes and chuckling. 'I never thought I'd see anything as corny as that in Oxford,' he replied.

John Morris repeated, in puzzlement, 'Corny? Is that good or bad?'

'Good,' George said. 'I was born in Nebraska.'

The joke was neither very good in its own right nor suitably chosen for an English listener, but it had an Olsen and Johnson flavour that was entirely in keeping with the tone of the evening.

My neighbours had shamed me into sweeping the sidewalk every day. However cold or blustery the weather, the wife of the pubkeeper scrubbed the pub steps every morning. Old Mrs Edward, a frail little body of eighty-plus, was just as reliable about tidying her section of the pavement, which adjoined ours. On this January morning she was finishing her chore when I— bundled in a duffle coat, wool cap, mittens, and fleece-lined boots —joined her. *Her* sweeping costume consisted of a wool cardigan over a cotton dress, and it made me colder just to look at her. We were having ten degrees of frost that day (Americans would call it twenty-two degrees above zero) yet she seemed perfectly comfortable, and even lingered for a moment after she'd swept the last gum wrapper into the gutter. The weather was beastly, didn't I agree?

I did. But even when I was most uncomfortable I had to admit that it wasn't so beastly as we had come to England prepared to endure. The many people who had warned us about England's 'dreadful winter cold' had neglected to specify degree and duration, and George and me, raised in the American Midwest, dreadful winter and cold meant weeks of near-zero temperature, blanketing snow, and icy winds. Oxford's worst is the palest imitation of that. Warm ocean currents keep winter temperatures relatively high—in the thirties or forties, which is nippy enough, goodness knows, if the air is humid and one's house is uninsulated. But it certainly isn't 'dreadful winter cold'.

The fact that none of our informants had adequately stressed was the changeability of English weather. For such a little island Great Britain has enormous variety: there can be a snowstorm raging in Kent and a spring rain falling eighty-five miles away in Berkshire. The daily weather reports in the newspapers are split into individual forecasts for six different districts. (Not that they appeared very different to a casual reader—they usually said there would be 'sunny intervals and scattered showers, probably cloudy later, with drizzle or rain spreading from the west.') The consequence of this changeability was that a given pattern of weather rarely lingered longer than a few days. Just about the time that a cold snap prompted the writing of some poor-little-me letters home, the temperature would rise and it would rain. The weather having thus moderated, the fact that our house was uninsulated no longer mattered so much, and this, in a nutshell, is why English houses are that way.

The English don't believe in storm windows, either. Which is silly, because newer houses are using sizable areas of glass (all single pane) instead of the little leaded windows of yore. In Minnesota people could freeze to death in such houses. In England, where indoor temperatures can easily be maintained at about twenty degrees above freezing, inhabitants just shiver and carry on. I suspect that those stiff upper lips of theirs are camouflage for chattering teeth.

Joan Wheare said that I was wrong, that there is real exhilaration in sliding between icy sheets toward the comforting discovery of a hot-water bottle at one's toes. And the distress of a certain Oxford don was genuine when it was proposed by the head that central heating be installed in one of the buildings at his college. 'But, Master,' he protested, '*then the whole building will be warm.*'

It's true, too, that the English are hardy. Babies get aired regardless of weather, and no amount of cold alters the wearing of short pants by little boys, even though their bare knees turn blue. They consider themselves warm if they have thick, woolly scarves around their necks. In rain only Americans and the infirm aged wear galoshes or rubbers. Furthermore, normal body temperature among the English, according to their household fever termometers, is 98.4—in contrast to America's 98.6, so maybe they *do* have a greater inbred tolerance to cold.

But I am not convinced that it's wholly a matter of physiology. There's still a strong streak of Puritanism in the English. They've convinced themselves that it's immoral to be too comfortable. Deprivation builds character. Chins up, lads, chilblains are *good* for you! At any rate, they couldn't have picked better spots for mortifying *my* flesh. The most uncomfortable room in most English houses is the cubicle where the toilet is installed, and the next coldest room is the bath. If cleanliness is next to godliness, I slipped from grace during the Oxford winter. It took more moral fibre than I possess to lower myself into the clammy embrace of a porcelain tub in an unheated bathroom, just on promise of having a warm towel when I got out.

That January, Oxford had a fair sampling of any kind of weather you'd care to name. It was both inspiriting and unsettling. There had been snow right after Christmas, not much, just enough to make inch-high caps on the gravestones in St Andrew's churchyard at the bottom of our street. Then rain. Then frost. Then frost with fog. (That was the worst; it bit to the marrow of the bones.) Then two brilliant days of hoar-frost, when the sun shone down from a cloudless, cold blue sky on a world that sparkled with diamond dust. Every blade of grass, every twig, every ivy leaf was rimmed with chalky white, and the whole landscape had an ethereal beauty I've never seen matched by either sleet or snow. Then rain again. And another bout of fog.

Our little pink house immediately reflected all changes in outside temperature, humidity, or wind direction, and it was impossible to maintain anything like an even moderate warmth inside. If, in mild weather, I turned off the stoves overnight, the temperature always seemed to drop and by morning the inside panes of the living-room windows would be faintly rimed. If there was a brisk wind, drafts shot across the floors or played around our shoulders, and if we cut their force by closing all room doors, the burning paraffin in rooms without cross-ventilation made us feel logy and gave us headaches. Finally I threw up my hands and decided that it was simpler just to keep the stoves going full blast all the time, opening windows as necessary to prevent anoxia. Mr Shergold the Headington ironmonger must have thought that we either bathed in or drank the vast quantities of paraffin he delivered, since no one could possibly have burned so much fuel.*

Whenever a day looked passable, and sometimes even when it didn't, we continued our sight-seeing. ('Neither snow, nor rain, nor heat, nor gloom of night . . .' applies to tourists, too.) We took Mother, one leaden Sunday, to Blenheim Palace, Churchill's birthplace. It had an austere and forbidding beauty, the great grey pile of stone that is called England's Versailles rising out of a snow-powdered park, the lovely gardens laid out by Capability Brown hidden from view, the lake turned steely grey and desolate. We also drove to Ewelme, whose watercress beds were a slash of brilliant green—of pulsing life in a near-dead world— and whose little church and ancient almshouses were as charming as we'd been told.

* On the other hand, these customers were Americans. And Americans *do* keep their rooms boiling hot.

It was there I saw my first tomb with the dear departed in sculptured stone, richly arrayed and serenely beautiful, atop the coffin; and in a narrow enclosure beneath the coffin an effigy of the same person in a simple shift, face wracked by pain and body emaciated by disease. A nice reminder, this, that fine robes and high position—this was a sixteenth-century Duchess of Suffolk's tomb—do not get one into heaven, and that in the end all men meet their Maker on equal footing.

On each of those January Sundays, Mother and I went to a different church. The Anglican churches were half empty; the English are not a nation of churchgoers. Although St Columba's Scottish Rite Presbyterian was packed, Headington Baptist (it was odd to hear such churches called 'non-conformist') had only a handful. They were working-class people in that congregation, scrubbed and tidy, and the only churchgoers of the lot who spoke to us, the strangers in their midst, after the service.

We didn't attend any services at what the English call 'the R.C. churches', but we went to St Andrews for Boy Scout Sunday, and its service was so high that only the Mass in English distinguished it from Roman Catholic. Wearing short-sleeved cotton shirts and corduroy shorts, the St Andrews Scouts sat together in the front rows of a church so cold one could see one's breath. Mother's attention drifted away from the service as she watched one little boy's lips turn blue. I was less concerned because I'd been in England longer and knew that he'd arrive home rosy, and perhaps even warm, after a lively run in the brisk January air. The scene from that service that remains brilliantly in my memory is how sudden sunlight streamed through the old stained glass into the choir, and how the clouds of incense floated lazily in the brightness like dust motes in the hot air of an August noon in California.

In town we dutifully 'did' a few of the colleges, but it was too cold to linger long in most of them. I suspect that my mother's enduring enthusiasm for New College chapel is a tribute not to its greater beauty but to the fact that she examined its details in greater comfort. It has radiators underneath the benches where tired sight-seers naturally sink down to rest.

Hilary term began in the third week of January, and although the high excitement and the frantic socialization of the first term had disappeared, the pulse of Oxford life quickened. As the undergraduates and dons returned from vacation, the city streets grew gay again, and the Carfax became once more an international crossroads.

Mother and I were en route to a luncheon one day, when a fashionable French lady boarded our town-bound Headington bus. Blonde as a biscuit from creamy angora hat to pointed pale beige slippers, she sputtered and waved her arms and she thrust a card at the bus conductress. The broad-beamed, ruddy-faced country girl read the address on the card, shifted her gum, patted Madame on the shoulder, and cheerily replied, 'Don't worry, love. We'll find it. Fi'pence ha'penny, please.'

As we waited in queue at the bus transfer point, we saw a tiny Indian lady in a bright sari and fleece-lined boots, pushing her brown baby in a pram like a galleon. A blue-black Nigerian and a red-bearded Scot, both with college scarves around their necks, overtook her, cut around her—one on each side—and continued their earnest conversation across the pram until they had forged ahead sufficiently to walk again side by side. Behind us, clustered at a shopwindow, were three Latin-American girls rolling their eyes and trilling their r's as they window-shopped for shoes. On the drab street, among the pale-faced English in dun-coloured clothes, the señoritas looked like goldfinches that had somehow wandered into a flock of sparrows.

'The only thing that's missing from this scene,' I said to Mother, 'is an undergraduate in a purple exercise suit running through town. They do it all the time—five or six mile runs, just for the fun of it.'

She agreed that it was all very exotic, and did I feel a slight drizzle beginning?

The days seemed very short now, because so rarely was there sun. One evening, homeward bound from a visit to St Edmund Hall—a kind of Lilliput among the colleges, with all their charms in miniature—Mother waved her hand (the one that wasn't carrying the umbrella) at the shrouded windows we were passing. 'They look so—so unfriendly. So withdrawn,' she said.

'It's just the English need for privacy,' I replied. 'It shocks them to see the way Americans leave their blinds up or their draperies undrawn. At least half a dozen people here—of those who've visited the States—have mentioned our lack of fencing,

and the way that lawns often blend into neighbouring lawns.
I suppose all that openness seems to them like pitiless exposure.'

'Speaking of exposure.' my mother said, 'I *do* wish you'd do
something about your bathroom window. Not even a casement
curtain over it.'

'Oh, I don't think anybody can see in,' I replied. 'The only
house in sight is way across the park. Besides, our view out is
awfully pretty. Even in winter.'

(Much, much later—just about the time we left England, in
fact—the thought occurred to me that maybe Mother Knew
Best. Perhaps the lady of that distant house was a bird watcher
equipped with binoculars. There had been certain indications
that walled houses and curtained windows don't mean the
absence of watchful eyes behind them. In the spring, sometime,
a neighbour casually mentioned that my husband had been out
working in the garden uncommonly early. I knew, from having
been shown through her house, that the only view of our garden
was from her cook's window, a dormer on the third floor. And
another neighbour asked if she might have the block of American
air-mail stamps from a fat letter we had just received. She knew
that we had them because the mailman had drifted into the
habit of showing off our mail to other people on his route. I think
now that the Englishman's sense of privacy is illusory.)

Early in February, Mother decided that winter's traces were
too long for *her* powers of endurance and that she'd do her
waiting for the hounds of spring in the civilized comforts of
steam-heated America. With her departure I settled down to
huge quantities of reading and occasional fits of self-pity. I had
developed an intermittent, deep-seated pain in my middle that
alarmed me. Maybe I had an ulcer. Or cancer. Red was a source
of worry too. He looked like a wrung-out chamois skin and was
just as limp. I plied him with eggnogs and fretted.

'Well, call the doctor and ask his advice,' George suggested.
'That's what we're paying him for.'

This was a jest, because—since we didn't pay taxes—Dr
Cullen's services didn't cost us one penny. In Great Britain everyone who applies for free medical care may have it, whether or
not he has paid a farthing into the common pot. And if some
Frenchmen pop across the Channel to get free dentures? Or
some Irish girls emigrate briefly to give birth to out-of-wedlock

babies? Ignore the free-loaders, the British reasoned when they set up the National Health Service: *It will be cheaper to treat those few who aren't legitimately entitled to the service than to keep detailed records for the many who are.* Earlier in the year, when we had filled out three lines on a three-by-five card and had thus become entitled to free medical care, we had recalled without nostalgia the forms in triplicate that we had filled out at home in order to apply for or collect medical insurance. We had thought, too, of the avalanche of paper work that buries employers, doctors, hospitals, and insurance companies in the States. I still don't understand how the same people who persist in such absurdities as putting water pipes on the outside walls of their houses could also have adopted such a brilliantly logical solution to the problem of administering with a minimum of red tape a programme of medical care for fifty million people.

As for the doctoring, it seemed fine. I *did* call Dr Cullen, as George had suggested, but since Red didn't have any alarming symptoms—just pallor and general lassitude—there wasn't much the doctor could prescribe beyond a nourishing diet and plenty of rest. Unless, of course . . .

'Dr Cullen, do you think that a course of vitamins might help to get the boy back on to his feet?'

No sooner had I voiced the question than I wanted to withdraw it. I had suddenly recalled a fragment of conversation I'd overheard at a coffee party. The speakers had been the wives of two doctors. One had said, 'Ian has a couple of new patients—Americans.' The other wife had groaned. Then both had laughed, and the first one had said, obviously mimicking, 'How about some vitamins'—only she pronounced it 'vittamins', English style—'and a shot, huh?' So I knew that preventive medicine of this sort isn't so fashionable in England as in the United States, and I wasn't surprised when Dr Cullen vetoed vitamins and recommended patience.

Then I went in to see him myself about the pain in my middle.

Sitting on a hard bench in his 'surgery'—which means office, not operating room—and clutching a number, as in a butcher shop back home, I waited no longer in his clinic-style outer office than I am accustomed to wait in doctors' offices at home. The difference in America is that you have an appointment. Also, the furnishings are more de luxe here, the magazines are slicker, there's a glamorous receptionist, and the doctor wears a white coat. English doctors sit behind their desks looking like loan officers in a bank.

Dr Cullen listened to the recital of my symptoms, made an examination, said that nothing seemed to be badly amiss, but that perhaps I should be examined by a specialist. One way you can identify an English doctor as a specialist is that he has dropped the label. Dr Cullen sent me to Mr Gray, an internist, as a private patient—which meant that I had to pay for his services.

Mr Gray took me thoroughly apart. Then he said, lifting a letter from a file, 'I concur in Dr Cullen's diagnosis.'

'Oh,' I asked, 'did he make one?'

'A hypothesis. But he wanted me to rule out other possibilities. I have done so.'

Here it comes, I thought. *Be brave.*

'You seem to have pulled a muscle in the diaphragm, Mrs Beadle. It will right itself in time. Unless, of course, you submit it to further stresses.'

And so it did. The pain in my middle went away soon after George and Red took over the job of toting in the heavy scuttles of coal for the Rayburn.

That's all the medical care I needed in England. So I'm no authority on socialized medicine. I *heard* that English doctors still don't like it much. But the public likes it fine, so I'm afraid the doctors are stuck with it.

Would it work in the United States? I suppose a pent-up demand for medical services would overwhelm our doctors just as it did the English ones when the plan first went into effect. But I also believe that Americans would *continue* to make more demands on their doctors than the English now do. Our attitude toward health is different—and it isn't just a matter of being more sold on vitamins and shots, either. There must be neurotics in England, as in my homeland, who consult doctors as a substitute for entertainment, but in general the English are less prone to worry about their health, take less elaborate precautions to protect it, and ignore minor illnesses to a much greater extent than we do.

Some 25 per cent of Oxford babies are still born at home—partly for lack of hospital facilities, but partly because a good many women prefer it that way; and the midwife, who in America supplies health care primarily for hillbillies and the indigent, has in England a respected and vital place in the medical hierarchy. It is assumed that English mothers are quite capable of ministering to all but the most catastrophic illnesses of their children, and there's much less folderol about sanitation. An English schoolteacher, doing a stint in an American school, reported her astonishment when a child dropped an unwrapped 'sweet' on the floor, to see the little girl pick up the candy and throw it into the wastebasket—instead of popping it into her mouth, as an English child would have done.

At Red's school, if a parent requested it, boys who had been ill were excused from participation in the compulsory Wednesday-afternoon games—but not from attendance. If they were well enough to be in class, they were well enough to go to the playing field, the masters reasoned. And since one got colder standing and watching a game than running with the pack, most youngsters with a dislike of sports didn't use the sniffles as an excuse to escape. Furthermore, this lack of pampering seemed to do children no particular harm. 'You've got a temperature, but you might well go back to class—you've had a temperature for months,' said a school nurse to one little American girl whose mother I knew. In general, most of the American children in Oxford got through their year in England with fewer ailments than at home.

Kitty Turnbull summed up this Spartan streak—at least for the distaff side—when she said, 'Women of other countries seem to go to bed when they feel unwell. We Englishwomen go for a brisk walk with the dogs.'

Chapter 10

IT WASN'T REALLY such a bad winter—seen from the vantage point of May. But at the time there seemed to be an awful lot of February and March. Spring was coming. You could see the signs: snowdrops blooming along the hedges, an early crocus or two, the lilac buds swelling. But spring itself remained out of reach, like a lollipop held frustratingly just beyond a child's grasp.

The snow and frost of January had been followed by a week of false spring, when the air grew balmy and people laid off their scarves; and everything that had been frozen suddenly thawed. Old walls all over Oxford collapsed—including a hunk of ours—and within a few days the entire Thames Valley was flooded. Meadows turned into ponds; ducks paddled through goal posts on school playing fields; drowned stalks of Brussels sprouts swayed gently in their watery graves—and everyone who had gotten flu in December promptly came down with it. Then the fog rolled in again. On February 17th the *Oxford Times* announced in boldface type that 'six minutes of sunshine were recorded in Oxford yesterday, the first time the sun has been seen since February 5th.' In between fog and frost and snow it rained. We all felt oppressed, and tired, and jumpy.

I tried to 'think positive'—and the negative thoughts loomed larger and blacker. Shopping had always been fun, because to look at the labels on canned goods and shipping crates was like a world tour: butter from Denmark, lamb from New Zealand, tomatoes from the Canaries, wine from Yugoslavia, oranges from South Africa or Israel. Now this game lost its allure, and all I could see at the market was the lack of celery or lettuce, or anything else crisp and green. Sometimes, at the city's one shop that catered to foreign tastes, I could find capsicums (green peppers), hothouse-grown in Israel, but they didn't allay the craving for something juicy.

It had always been a sporting challenge to hunt for a pair of shoes or a blouse in both the correct size and desired style, but now I grew cross because the English refuse to learn the mechanics of stock control. I very nearly reduced to tears the gentle little shopgirls who say, with such sweet apology, 'I'm sorry, madam. We seem to be out just now.' (Heavens, it isn't *their* fault.)

I got picky about workmanship and refused to pay the window washer for an especially slovenly job. Until then the fact that the average English workman has no pride of craft had been a mild astonishment (since I had expected the reverse), but essentially unimportant. After all, unlike my Oxford housewife friends, I wasn't going to have to live permanently in a house like theirs—with linoleum laid in humps and wallpaper carelessly matched and paint dribbles at the corners of the mouldings. But now, suddenly, I found myself taking shoes back to the cobbler for 'a proper job of stitching.' I thumped around after Mrs Blount, finding fault with the way she did the corners. And I told Red that if he didn't find another barber I was going to cut his hair myself, I was sick and tired of his looking as if he'd kept his hat on while his hair was being cut. (Actually there were some pretty good barbers in Oxford; Red had simply picked a bad one. His nickname in the trade was Slasher Slade.)

There is almost always a funny side to irksome situations, but in February and March I couldn't seem to see it. I was outraged instead of amused when a jeweller on the High Street, whom I had asked to estimate the cost of restringing a pearl necklace, held the remnants of the strand between two fingers—as if it were a decaying fish—and said, with consummate distaste, 'These, madam, are *paste*.' Dammit, I knew they were paste. I just wanted an estimate on how much it would cost to restring them.

My chronic feud with the laundry that did George's shirts—every housewife in England has a feud with her laundry—erupted into permanent estrangement. I knew that the Royal Rose had outmoded equipment, that many of its workers were ill with flu, and that its proprietors deserved my patient understanding. I had survived the capricious changing of delivery and pickup dates, and the starching of handkerchiefs and bath towels, and had even found a small measure of excitement, when opening each week's bundle, in seeing whose clothes were mixed in with mine this time. What finished me off was the time of year and the addition to George's shirts of a gimmick borrowed from the United States. His shirts, which went to the laundry with buttons wherever buttons should be, had always come back with most of the buttons missing; I was used to *that*. What infuriated me now was that the laundry took to sewing on one button, then slipping over it a tag that said, 'This button was missing and has been replaced by the Royal Rose Laundry.'

The roof sprang a leak and the man who promised to repair it never showed up. The second man who promised to repair it came the day after he had said he would, then left a huffy note because nobody had been home to admit him. The remaining apples in Blaze's 'ouse began to spoil; and the only surviving geranium plant in the solarium quietly shed its two remaining leaves and expired. The fridge—which had been wheezing alarmingly for several months—finally went conk; and the damp spots on the wallpaper rose another foot above the baseboards.

Oh, I was loaded for bear, all right, the day the phone went dead.

'And what about the telephone listing and bills?' I had asked Lady Headington when we had moved in.

'It will be easier to keep the listing in my name,' she had said. 'And I've given the telephone people instructions to send the bills to Mr Bennett at Balliol.'

This struck me as odd, and the domestic bursar had confirmed my view. The rent he paid, yes, but not the utilities.

Therefore, I had telephoned the telephone company. (As an Oxford newcomer, I had not yet learned that Oxford's preferred way of communication is to write a letter.) Accounts had informed me that our phone number, Oxford 61840, would have to be carried in our landlady's name since it could be transferred to our name only with her permission, and she had by then left for Africa. Accounts would, however, see to it that we were listed with Directory Enquiries as a second user of 61840. And, finally, Accounts had said that they 'most certainly did *not* have instructions to send the bill to the domestic bursar at Balliol; that would be most irregular.'

So we had relaxed, used the phone, and made a kind of uneasy truce with it. We soon grew accustomed to male operators on the night shift, but we had never ceased to long for the speedy American 'Number, please?' We stewed and fretted while waiting for the operator to answer; while holding one end of what was obviously an open wire but that remained mute during the long minutes when the operator was presumably making the connection; while trying to converse against background fireworks; and while trying to rouse somebody, anybody, on the frequent occasions when a lifted receiver produced no dial tone, no voices, no nothing at all. The last circumstance we had come to attribute to the Other Party on the Line, whose children either took the phone off the hook or who removed it herself during their nap time so the dears wouldn't be disturbed.

English phone bills are rendered at six-month intervals, by which time, of course, the sum can be staggering, but what had surprised us more than the amount of our first phone bill (in January) was that it had been sent to the domestic bursar at Balliol. Mr Bennett had promptly forwarded it to us, and we had as promptly paid it. I had no doubt of this fact until one day in March. At 8.30 that morning I lifted the receiver in order to place a call to London. Getting no response, I assumed that the Other Party on the Line had left the receiver off the hook again. *Those children!* I thought. At 9 a.m. the situation was unchanged, and at 10 a.m., and 10.30. So it was in no gentle mood that I stamped next door and asked a neighbour if I might use her telephone in order to report that mine was out of order, and to place my London call.

First I called Faults and Service Difficulties. No answer. Faults and Service Difficulties was probably putting on the water for her eleven-o'clock cup of tea.

Then I dialled Operator and placed my call to London, saying that although I was calling from 62389 I wanted the call charged to 61840, my own number, which appeared to be out of order.

'One minute, please,' said the operator, and vanished from the line. I shifted the receiver into my other hand, opened my coat, and leaned against the wall in my neighbour's hallway.

When the operator cut in again, she said, 'I'm afraid I can't bill the call to 61840, madam. It's out of service.'

'I know it is,' I replied. 'That's why I'm calling from 62389. I've tried to report that 61840 is out of order, and I'll try again as soon as I've gotten this London call through. Meanwhile, however, I *would* like to be connected with London.'

The operator was patient and courteous. '61840 is not out of order, madam. It's out of service. Inoperable.'

'Inoperable?' I asked. 'Why?'

'I'll connect you with Enquiries, madam.'

While waiting this time I caught a fragment of another subscriber's telephone conversation. This is also par for the course in making an Oxford phone call. The trouble with it is you never hear enough—just '. . . black bile and all that vomiting . . .' and then the voices fade away.

Enquiries came on the line. 'Why is my phone, 61840, not working?' I asked. Enquiries told me that 61840 was out of service. 'That's right,' I said, and I could feel my blood pressure rising. My voice had already risen. 'I *know* it's out of service. WHY?'

Enquiries left the line. On cutting in again she said I'd best talk to Accounts.

The knowledge that I was about to talk to Accounts put me immediately on the defensive. Had the phone company deliberately cut off our service? If so, non-payment could have been the only reason. But we'd paid our bill. Promptly. Hadn't we? Certainly. Well, almost certainly . . .

Then I remembered that the cheque book was in my purse. I fished into it, got the cheque book, and riffled the pages. (This is not an easy job one-handed, while clutching the receiver of a wall telephone, in a dark hallway.)

I dropped the cheque book just as the operator came back on the line.

'Are you there?'

'Yes,' I said in a small, meek voice ready to eat crow.

The line went dead again.

I retrieved the cheque book, found the January entries, found the record of payment. We *had* paid. O.K. Whatever the trouble was, it wasn't non-payment.

Accounts came on the line. She informed me that 61840 was out of service because the bill had not been paid.

'WHAT?' I yelped, now suffused with righteous wrath. 'I have my cheque book in hand. We paid you on January 22nd.'

Not the January bill, Accounts replied. The February bill.

'No February bill has been rendered,' I snapped.

Oh yes, one had been, said the Voice with the Smile, only she was having to work at it now. 'It was for an overseas call. We bill those separately. However, the bill was returned to us by the post office. Undeliverable to the subscriber at that address, I believe. The subscriber is no longer in residence, I believe?'

'Yes, that's right,' I said. 'She's in Africa. But we—'

'It is unwise'—and now the Accounts' voice had taken on a faintly disapproving tone—'to leave a telephone in service in an unoccupied house, madam. Someone might break in and use it.'

'But the house *is* occupied. Or are you suggesting that *we* have broken in and are occupying it illegally?' (There was a horrified gasp at the other end of the line.) 'We rent it from the subscriber. What's more, you people are perfectly well aware of the fact. When we took the house, we arranged that we should be listed at this number too. As second users of the phone.'

'Oh, but that listing would be in Directory Enquiries, madam. This is Accounts.'

I took a deep breath. I was beginning to feel weary. Then a new thought struck me. 'Besides, I don't see how the bill could have been marked undeliverable, and returned, because you haven't been billing the subscriber at this address, anyway. You send the bills to the domestic bursar at Balliol, he sends them to us, and we pay you. Or at least that's how the January bill was handled.'

There was a long pause. When she spoke, Accounts' voice was very frosty. 'I'm afraid that would be most irregular, madam.'

I fought for control. Then, very slowly, I said, 'All right. Let's skip all that for the moment. Tell me just one thing: how do I go about getting my phone to work again?'

'We'll be most happy to release the line, madam, now that we know the house is occupied. Shall we render another bill, madam?'

'Yes. And address it this time to Beadle, will you? B-E-A-D-L-E. Now, can I make that London call? And charge it to 61840?'

'Certainly, madam.' She was all brisk and efficiency again. 'I'll give the operator the neccessary clearance.'

So I placed my call again, including the request that it be billed to 61840. The operator bounced right back with the information that 61840 was out of service, and therefore she couldn't charge the call to that number.

I banged the phone down, went up the street, and placed the call from a public pay phone. I was so angry that the friend I was calling said later I sounded like a sergeant-major *ordering* her to have lunch with me the following day, when I expected to be in the city.

Then I lifted the receiver again, intending to call somebody—anybody—in the main office of the telephone company, and blow his head off. But the thought occurred that I'd had conspicuous lack of success thus far in transacting business with the telephone company on the telephone. So I hopped the next bus and went downtown to see the telephone company in person.

I was taken care of by a genial Scot named Drummond. He settled me solicitously in a comfortable chair. He asked if he could fetch me a cup of tea. He listened to my tale and made copious notes. He sent a messenger to Accounts to get the file on 61840. He sympathized with my annoyance. He knew exactly how I felt, having himself been recently dunned for three pounds that, it turned out, was owed the merchant in question by a man named Diamond. This was a shocking thing, really, since he, Drummond—like myself—had a horror of being in debt and had always paid his bills promptly. Finally he conceded that the telephone company had been 'a wee bit inefficient.' But, on the other hand, 'The subscriber had really ought not to have kept the phone in her name if the bills were to be paid by someone else.' Then he escorted me to the door, thanking me for my promptness in bringing the matter to his attention. I found myself apologizing for having taken up his time on such a trivial matter.

Our next telephone bill—the closing one—came to us in the United States eleven months after we had left England. It had been sent to the domestic bursar at Balliol.

At noon, on one late March Sunday, the air felt surprisingly warm. We could feel sun through the mist, and George suddenly said, 'Let's get out of here.'

We went to Coventry, partly because it was close enough for a half-day trip and partly because someone had said to me, when I had been less than enthusiastic about the modern architecture I had seen in England, '*Do* go to Coventry, then. The new cathedral is quite good.'

Nothing about the approaches to the city—miles of red brick houses and modern factories—resembled the environs of that other city George and I had once visited, half a world away, which had also been virtually obliterated by one bombing raid. Yet parallels with Hiroshima were inescapable: both cities are almost treeless at the centre; both are rebuilding in a modern style at odd variance with surviving pre-war architecture; and both have preserved fragments of bombed buildings as permanent war memorials. Hiroshima's was once a museum, the framework of its original dome traced now by a skeleton of rusted steel. Coventry's is the spire and ravaged walls of its ancient cathedral.

From the city square, with its prim grey statue of Lady Godiva, we could see the cathedral's frilly fifteenth-century spire, a visual feast in rosy stone. It looked much the same as many another spire in many another English city, and the approach was the same—through a network of narrow little streets that afforded no long view of what lay ahead. The air was gentle, and Sunday lassitude lay over the town. Hence, nothing prepared us for the shock of finding ourselves, abruptly and violently, in a ruin.

Of the cathedral itself, only one row of windows is left. A few bits of glass cling to the mullions. The dome of the sky is now the roof of the cathedral. Stumps of pillars remain to mark the centre aisle, and gravelled paths and plots of grass have replaced the floor.

The nave remains. Where once the altar stood, laid with fine cloth and holy vessels, a rough stone altar now stands. It was constructed from the ruins by an elderly stonemason who had been the cathedral's night fire watcher. On the centre of this altar is a huge charred cross, made from half-burned beams that fell from the roof into the church during the raid, in 1941, that nearly destroyed Coventry. Behind the altar, following the curve of the apse, is a legend in gold. It says, 'Father, Forgive.'

As tourists, we are great chatterboxes. I like to spin fantasies about the people who once inhabited a place. Red sees to it that I stick to the facts; it annoys him for me to populate a Tudor castle with Stuarts. And George discusses camera angles. But in the ruins of Coventry Cathedral we were all silent. It was like being at a funeral.

Over to the left, in line with the transept of the original

cathedral, the handsome new cathedral was then abuilding. It lacked the porch that by now has linked it to the ruins of the old cathedral, but it was easy to visualize the eventual unity of the two. Standing in the ruins, one looks up the centre aisle of the new cathedral all the way to the altar. And vice versa: as worshippers leave a service, the ruins ahead underline the fact that men have yet some distance to travel if brotherhood in God is their aim.

Out in the ruined church, exposed now to the weather, are many of the memorial plaques that once lined the interior walls. The one I noted in particular was put up in the twenties 'to the glorious memory of the officers and men of the Royal Warwickshire Regiment who fell in the Great War.' That was the war to end wars. Remember? Yet twenty years after that memorial to the fallen of World War I had been dedicated, Coventry was in flames.

As the roof burned off the cathedral, and the pillars collapsed, and a hailstorm of steel and stone filled the air, the bronze of the plaque was slashed like tissue paper. The torn metal curled back a little, and in consequence several letters in the inscription cannot be seen. It doesn't matter. Out in the open as it is, and with that gaping wound across its face, the message comes through loud and clear.

As we were tiptoeing out of the ruins, I glanced back. Behind the outdoor altar, and beyond the legend in gold, was a bed of crocuses. A toddler, straying from his parents, had wandered over to the flowers and had bent to pick, or perhaps to smell, one. His mother caught sight of him just as I did.

'Alfie!' she called in horrified tones. '*Alfie!* Leave off that!'

Alfie's lip quivered, but he stood his ground. I don't know whether he picked, or smelled, his crocus. What I'd *like* to know is whether his generation will do better by the world than mine has.

Chapter 11

THERE IS a theatrical trick in which a scrim curtain is hung between audience and stage, a curtain that is opaque until the scene behind it is lit. Side lights first pick out one small section of the stage; then another; and then another. Next, the back and top lights begin to brighten the entire scene. One's sense of anticipation builds and builds, until—crescendo!—the footlights go full up and the curtain rises, and the audience bursts into joyous applause.

That's what our English spring was like.

The little earth-hugging flowers came first, in late February. Snowdrops bloomed in drifts under trees and hedges; then the crocuses thrust their shiny heads above the earth; later, the woods were hazy with bluebells. In March the forsythia opened its yellow trumpets, followed, in quick succession, by the rosy plums, the white cherries, and the pale pink apple blossoms. In April the chestnuts began to unfold, wrinkled and tender, from their furry buds and by May they were studded with white flowering spikes as jaunty as candles on a Christmas tree. In contrast, the laburnums, their pendant yellow clusters like showers of golden rain, curved earthward with willow-plate grace. The tulips bloomed and waned and dropped their velvety petals among the scillas. Wistaria cloaked grey walls in mauve, lilacs echoed the note against a backdrop of green, and here and there a vine of clematis blushed pink.

The rooks held noisy congress in the tree tops, and householders with small paint pots in hand ventured from hibernation to lay fresh trims on outside woodwork. Prams turned up on the streets with fringed cotton-print canopies, the babies inside wiggling bare pink toes, the mothers exposing winter-white shoulders to the sun.

Oh, it was good to be alive in England, now that spring was there! It was a time for flexing the muscles, opening the windows, airing the bedding, and smiling at strangers. It was a time for going outdoors and staying there.

On the first of May we arose at 4.30 a.m. and set out for Magdalen Bridge, afoot, in predawn grey. The fields were cool and wet, the air like glass, and the only sound was a cuckoo's call somewhere up ahead of us. I'd forgotten that cuckoos are birds, not clock parts; their song, at least in the hush of a spring morning twilight, has a wistful sweetness and clarity that is almost painful to hear.

As the footpath we were following eased off to the north, we swung back toward London Road, and joined it just as it began its descent down Headington hill. It was after 5 a.m. now, and we were no longer alone. Schoolboys in twos and threes whizzed by on their bikes, and coveys of schoolgirls giggled past us downhill, the bright ribbons on their straw boaters floating behind them. Some had wound wreaths of flowers around their hatbrims. This rite of spring we were headed for seemed to be a young folks' festival.

It takes the stamina of youth, or an unquenchable taste for romance, to arise before dawn—or to stay up past it, as some of the crowd that was awaiting us on Magdalen Bridge had done. As we eased our way into the heart of the throng, we could see that the river was just as full as the bridge.

Undergraduates and town boys, mutually seizing the one annual opportunity to escape the restraints of proctors and policemen, had been up all night, partying on the Cherwell. Now they were jammed into punts, and the punts were jammed so close together that the merrymakers were using them as stepping stones to cross the river. A snatch of calypso drifted up to us on the bridge. If one looked carefully, one could see an occasional champagne cork go pop. There were beer mugs, too, but they were being used as balers.

On the far side of the bridge, soaring 140 feet above the lot of us, stood Magdalen College Tower—cold and grey against the blue-white sky, its clock hands gleaming dully in the early light. Red spotted a flutter of white near its top. 'Look,' he whispered (I don't know why, a yell would have gone unnoticed), 'there are the choirboys.'

Just then a ray of sunlight touched the pinnacles atop the

tower. And the clock began to strike. The hundreds on the bridge fell silent. By the sixth stroke the pinnacles were all alight. Then, like an angel chorus, faint and sweet, the voices of the choirboys floated down to us. 'Te Deum Patrem Colimus' they sang, as has been the Oxford custom for five hundred years —on this day, from this tower, at sunup.

(They have not always had such an attentive audience. In the nineteenth century town boys would stand on the bridge, beating on the tubs and blowing horns to drown out the hymn. And the angel chorus, ammunition cached under those spotless robes, would race through the song, then rush to the parapet and pelt the town boys with rotten eggs. But as we of the polite twentieth century stood listening, the only sound was a splash and a muffled yell from the river. Someone had obviously fallen off a punt.)

Then, as the last note of the hymn died away, the college bells began to peal out rich and full—the same glorious medley of sound we'd heard on Christmas Eve, only now the bells were saluting the sun and spring and life and love. They made our juices rise. They set the crowd moving—at a run

We surged up the High Street, like water escaping a dam. Past Magdalen itself. Past Queen Caroline, unshakably composed beneath her classic cupola at Queen's. Down the little lane beside St Mary's, all of us pushing and shoving and grinning at each other. Into Radcliffe Square. We ringed the grassy plot behind the church, but left it bare.

And here came the Morris Men, to fill it; here they came jigging into the square! In the van were the flute, the fiddle, and the concertina. And pretty girls with flowers and ribbons twined in their hair. The men were all in white, with flower-garlanded hats, red and blue ribbons crossed on their chests, ribbon armbands, bells and bows on their trousers. And how they danced! Most were young—Morris dances are not for weaklings—but here and there a snowy thatch emerged as a dancer removed his flowery hat to mop his brow and wipe the sweat off his bifocals. The University Morris Men had a turn, and then the dancers from Headington Quarry, and then the Oxford Morris Men. Leaping. Twirling. White scarves snapping. Hat ribbons whirling in horizontal orbits, wooden staves cracking like pistol shots. All the feet in the square tapped time.

Pirouetting on the edge of the grass, the man who was cast as the Hobby Horse bobbed the head of his silly steed. The walking tree called Jack-in-the-Green ambled in his blind and stately way from side to side, we in the crowd grabbing at the chicken-wire cone that encased him, trying to strip off his chestnut leaf cover. But his champion, the Jester, stuck close: leaping and prancing, his red and purple coattails jingling, he whacked our plucking fingers (and a head or two!) with his skin balloon.

And then the man with the gingerbread sword distracted us further. Packed into the hilt of his ancient cutlass was ginger cake. 'Have a bit,' he told us as he passed the sword along. 'Even a crumb will bring good health until next year.'

'If you live, that is,' called a voice from the crowd. A wave of laughter rewarded the sally. How *good* we all felt!

The Morris Men exited dancing and jigging and dipping out of the square, round the bend, and into the Broad. Some of us couldn't bear to let them go. We followed along, half-dancing ourselves, as bemused as if the Pied Piper were up ahead. ('*Mom!* For gosh sakes, come back on the sidewalk!')

By now the sun had fully risen, and suddenly we began to yawn—especially those among us who'd been up all night. School children started to scoot home to change into uniform. The big red buses began to grind past, discharging ordinary mortals on their way to work, their placid faces untouched by May magic. And little by little we early birds withdrew into our everyday shells, went home, and took up everyday tasks.

But even now—two years later, and six thousand miles away— I can still hear, faintly, the sound of the flute and the jingle of bells. I hear it more clearly than the roar of trucks going past a little pink house in Headington or the dull throb of cars and buses tangled at the Carfax.

Oxford has another rite of spring in May: Eights Week, with its bumping races on the river.

For a few the racing days are energetic days. For most they are lazy, sit-on-the-riverbank days. Everyone comes: mothers with babies in prams; school children on bikes; Old Boys with shooting sticks and field glasses; dons looking mostly undonnish with their noisy young in tow. Undergraduates, peonies or irises nodding from the lapels of their college blazers, strut about. Or bask in the warmth of winsome smiles from pretty girls in picture hats. (One thinks of peacocks with their hens.)

We went to the races, too, on a breezy afternoon, joining the crowd on the towpath below Folly Bridge. This is a stretch of the Thames that is called the Isis, as befits a town that venerates the classics. There was a busy trade in ferrying people across the river in large, flat-bottomed punts; the objective of most was a college boathouse or barge, above which heraldic college flags snapped briskly in the wind. The atmosphere was as gay and bustling and as fraught with expectation as a medieval tournament. Only the swans, shooed into the reeds along the race course, were argumentative and sulky.

We found a good spot on a bridge near a bend, midway in the mile-and-a-half course. Starting at intervals of a few seconds, the college eights in each race try to catch, and bump, the boat ahead. We had fine luck that day. We witnessed a bump. It happend like this:

The Hertford Eight came surging into view. This was not a competition between the picked rowing men of the universities, like the famous Oxford-Cambridge race at Putney; but even so, the Hertford boat cut through the water with so much grace it was hard to believe that the oarsmen were working as hard as they were.

Right on their heels was Lincoln.

Partisans of both colleges came running along the towpath, dodging prams and knocking over untended bicycles, firing pistols (blanks), and shouting encouragement to their men.

The Hertford cox, sensing peril, shortened the stroke. Backs bending, oars flashing, the lead boat spurted ahead. But two could play *that* game, and soon the Lincoln bow almost imperceptibly began to overlap the stern of its quarry.

A great roar went up on the riverbanks.

Then the Lincoln cox gave his rudder a gentle flick. His bow just nudged the flank of his prey. No more was needed: he'd made his kill.

The two boats drifted off to one side, Lincoln now a rung higher on its way toward becoming Head of the River.

Although a few dutiful cries of 'Well rowed, Hertford!' floated to the panting oarsmen from their supporters on the riverbanks, the fickle crowd was already intent on the next boats to come swooping along: St. Peter's, as it happened, with Jesus in hot pursuit. (I'm happy to report that neither suffered the indignity of a bump.)

And so it goes, with perhaps seven races a day and ten boats in each race, the starting positions shifting about each day in accordance with who did the bumping and who got bumped. Gala 'bump suppers' at college reward teams with four bumps to their credit, and on the Monday after it's all over and the swans have possession of the river again, the newspapers sum it all up for another year: —

Balliol, who on the first day of the Summer Eights had ousted Queen's from the Head of the River, were never in any danger of losing their place. Merton looking promising, but on Friday they faded, and were caught at the New Cut by a strong but rough Christ Church, who were the only crew in the first division to make their four bumps.

Long afterward, however, the rowing men will continue to argue whether, if the current hadn't been running quite so swiftly when they came out of the Gut. . . .

May, as I said, was a time for going outdoors and staying there. May was a time for walking.

To the west of Oxford, a few miles, is Port Meadow. This flat stretch of pastureland has been owned since before the Magna Carta by the freemen of the city of Oxford. Close by it are the ruins of Godstow Nunnery. There, Fair Rosamund lies buried. If you wish to break your walk, you can stop at The Trout for a glass of ale, and watch the river churn white at your feet as it tumbles through the weir.

Shotover Hill is to the east. Along its ridge is the road that Elizabeth followed when she visited Oxford in 1592; it's the same road that the beaten Royalists took after surrendering to Cromwell in 1646. It's a high road; you look above and beyond the spires and towers of Oxford to a green sea of tree tops and rolling farmland.

South-west, on the Lambourn Downs, in the Vale of the White Horse, there is another hill—this one surmounted by a vast earthen rampart thrown up by Bronze Age Britons. At the top, where the wind whips you hair and stings your eyes shut and flattens the grass as it surges downhill, the view is wilder and wider-spread, and the sky seems vast.

Yes, May was a good time for walking. May was a time to remember.

That was the spring of the great Latin debate, at both Oxford and Cambridge. I don't know what the atmosphere was like at Cambridge, but it was on the acrimonious side at Oxford. Blood ran as hot and tempers flared as fiercely as at any ball-park rhubarb in the States.

It was the scientists at both universities who had spearheaded the drive to drop the examination in Latin that was required for admission to either. It was important, furthermore, that the two institutions should make the same decision on the matter. Not that anyone dared insult the 'independence' of either university by suggesting that they get together on the problem; it was necessary to rely, instead, on their mutuality of interest and similarity of outlook, and hope that, as so often before, they would muddle through to a similar policy.

The fundamental similarity of the two great British universities, alone in the world in their organization around autonomous colleges and the tutorial system, is recognized by the English in common reference to them as one entity called 'Oxbridge'. They have equal prestige, and jointly are the mecca for the best young brains in the commonwealth; yet individually they are in hot competition with each other. To keep them well matched is essential. It would serve no useful purpose if their entrance requirements were fundamentally different, and it would cause a lot of agony.

Suppose that young Jonathan Bull, just going into the sixth form at his secondary school, has been so keen on science since he was twelve that he is clearly destined for the laboratory. If Oxford were to require a pass in Latin but Cambridge would let him in without it, he might be sorely tempted to prepare for Cambridge—dropping Latin in his last year or two of secondary school and taking more maths or one of the modern foreign languages that would be useful to him in science. This better background for science would clearly give him an advantage (at Cambridge) over schoolmates who were playing their cards more cautiously and were continuing to take Latin; so, in due course, the best scientific brains in Britain might end up at Cambridge. This would be unhealthy specialization, for academic institutions not engaged solely in research but also in educating youth should include in their fellowship a broad range of interests and points of view. On the other hand, if by some chance young Jonathan *didn't* make it at Cambridge, his lack of Latin would have disqualified him for consideration by Oxford. The secondary schools would thus find themselves in a difficult spot: which boys should they advise to take Latin and which should they advise to risk skipping it? It is hard enough, at present, to coach pupils for the small differences in qualifications that exist between the two universities.

Suppose the other alternative, now: the elimination of the Latin requirement by *both* universities. This would profoundly affect the secondary-school curriculum, the number of Latin masters needed, perhaps even the textbook business. So the great Latin debate at Oxbridge was more than a high wind blowing through the groves of Academe, and all of educated Britain followed with interest as the dons chose sides.

One hears at Oxford that the scientists have taken over Cambridge. And at Cambridge it's said that the philosophers have it pretty much their own way at Oxford. Such a claim is patently ridiculous: in institutions so decentralized that college bursars can't even co-operate to the extent of buying their light bulbs in job lots, it would be impossible for any special-interest group to dominate the others. More to the point, however, it isn't true. Although one Oxford scientist insists bitterly that Oxford has a 'redundancy of old men who sit about sipping port and discussing the meaning of meaning,' it seemed to us that Cambridge has quite enough medieval historians and theologians to meet Oxford eye to eye. As for science, George found that good research and teaching are going on at both institutions—with the same variations of excellence among the various scientific departments that are characteristic of all universities anywhere.

Cambridge struck me as a little more able to make up its collective mind than Oxford, but that opinion is based only on the outcome of the great Latin debate.

At both universities, of course, both pros and cons had been heard in a flow of impassioned oratory. The pro-Latinists had said that Latin is of inestimable value in understanding English and that familiarity with a classical language is an essential component of all true culture, indispensable to any man who wishes to call himself educated. The anti-Latinists had said that Latin grammar 'attains a pitch of arbitrary whimsicality far beyond the reach of mere disorder'; that 'no serious student of the matter would regard the influence of Latin upon understanding of English as anything but bad'; and that schoolboys would presumably still become familiar enough with Latin (below the advanced-pass level) to acquire whatever cultural benefits might be its to confer.

A humorous footnote to the whole business was that Latin, regardless of its fate as an entrance requirement, remains the official Oxbridge university language. Dons voted either *placet*—'It is pleasing'—or *non placet*; and at Cambridge they had decided, with little public fuss and by a sizable majority (325 *placets* to 278 *non placets*), that in the future candidates might be admitted 'without necessarily qualifying in a classical language.'

Matters had not proceeded quite so smoothly at Oxford. At Cambridge voting is by written ballot, but at Oxford the *placets* walk through one door and the *non placets* through another, with proctors on each side counting them as if they were livestock going into pens. George (who had cast his vote with the *non placets*) said that it had been a tense meeting indeed, because the line of gown-clad dons queued up at the two doors had looked so nearly equal. The final score was 249 *placets* to 244 *non placets*. Not that it really mattered, because Oxford had almost immediately reversed itself, reopened the entire matter, and debated it further. The hot potato had been disposed of, finally, by referring it to a committee for further study.

Which is where matters stood that spring when we went to Cambridge—George to give a lecture, I to see the sights. There was, of course, much conversation at Cambridge about the nature of Oxford's final decision. There was an off-chance that the older university just might . . . ('There always is, don't you know? Home of lost causes and all that.') But the consensus was that Oxford would eventually come around. It was unthinkable that the two universities would not again act in concert on a fundamental decision that affected them equally.

(Which is what happened, in case you're curious to know how it all came out. Some nine months later Oxford's committee

recommended to Congregation that an advanced-level pass in a
classical language should be dropped *only* for candidates holding
an advanced-level pass in mathematics or a scientific subject.
Anyone intending to read history or economics or modern languages must still come to Oxford with an advanced-level pass in
Latin or Greek. As a Rhodes scholar in residence at the time
put it, 'Mathematicians or scientists who feel the need of the
humanities on the side, as many of them do, will be free to choose
Pushkin instead of Vergil. Everyone else who reads Pushkin
must do it in addition to Vergil.')

Meanwhile, it was spring in Cambridge; they'd made *their*
decision; and how would we like to have a stroll through the
Fellows' Garden? Punting on the Cam, we'd find, was just as nice
as punting on the Cher.

Cambridge is a prettier university town than Oxford, because
it has no Morris Works. A number of colleges back up to the
river, their gardens overlooking it, and we strolled bemused on
paths that wander through these Backs. Nothing that we saw
in England was lovelier than Trinity College's living 'Persian
carpet'. Picture this: on either side of a path, two straight young
columns of pale green lime trees (Americans would call them
lindens) marched to the river. At a distance of twenty feet on
each side, a column of white cherry trees shimmered in full
bridal flower, their dropped petals spangling the earth below
them like confetti. Randomly spotted in the strip of meadow
grass between the two lines of trees, red tulips on sturdy stems
thrust bold heads to the sky; and nestled at their feet were daisies,
early buttercups, and baby blue-eyes, each adding a tiny fleck of
colour to the tapestry.

When George went off to do his lectures and lab tours, I
wandered through the colleges, then to the Church of the Holy
Sepulchre. It dates from 1100 and is round; the vicar said that it
had been built in imitation of the Holy Sepulchre in Jerusalem,
probably by the Knights Templar as a place of prayer for those
engaged in the Crusades. As I stood under the massive Norman
pillars and compact rounded arches, it was easy for me to transport myself to the time of Richard the Lion-Heart, and to get
at least a glimmer of the unquestioning faith of those earlier
Christians.

And, finally, on a windy, light-and-shadow kind of afternoon, with white clouds racing in battalions overhead, I visited Ely. Nowhere in England did I see a cathedral so impressive at a distance and so enthralling in its details, nor, oddly enough, one that struck me as so showy—as if several generations of bishops had been engaged in keeping up with the Joneses—and, in sum, so lacking in emotional impact.

I drove out with Mrs Severs, the wife of a Cambridge don. At first she tried gamesmanship, but as my questions continued to flow, she threw in the towel. 'I've never been here before either,' she confessed. We both laughed, agreed that one never *does* see the wonders in one's own back yard until visitors force one into it, and proceeded companionably, as fellow tourists.

The area north-east of Cambridge was once marshland in the centre of which a wide mound of dry ground rose like an island out of a sea. Although the fens were drained hundreds of years ago, the area is still called the Isle of Ely (the 'Ely' from the eels that once abounded there). And to travel over that flat expanse of countryside, especially under a turbulent sky, and to glimpse the vast bulk of the cathedral on the hill ahead, was like seeing a beacon on a dark and lonely night when one is lost.

Although the present cathedral dates from within a few years of the Norman Conquest, a couple of doors ornamented with the rugged zigzag and dogtooth carving of the period being particular treasures, much has been added. I thought that the additions had gilded the lily, but wandered from one to another in a state of exhilaration at their individual perfections. The wooden ceilings are painted in bright colours, those over the transepts having a spirited heavenly host in wood carvings that jut out into space as vigorously as figureheads on the prow of a ship. There's a fifteenth-century chapel with such frilly pinnacles and such intricate stone carving it looks as if the whole of Magdalen College Tower has been compressed into forty square feet. Under the seats of the choir stalls is a series of exquisite wood carvings, many of them domestic scenes from the fourteenth century. In short, everywhere you look, there is abundant evidence that the finest artists and craftsmen of the day—whatever the century— had given of their best. Guidebooks in hand, Mrs Severs and I looked with special awe at a dimly perceived ceiling carving of Christ—for which one John of Burwell earned two shillings and his meals at the prior's table, back in 1346.

The glory of Ely is its Octagon and Lantern. To visualize it, think first of a church built in the form of a cross, as they always were in the Middle Ages, with a tower in the centre where the transepts met the nave. In 1322 this tower at Ely collapsed. The ruin was absolute. Yet out of it came a tower that modern engineers marvel at. New pillars were inserted at the meeting of nave and transepts, eight sets of them, with walls between, to make an octagonal base for the new tower. The diameter of this octagonal space was seventy-four feet—too wide to arch stone— so they got some enormous beams and angled them out from the pillars like the ribs of an umbrella. Instead of letting them meet in the centre, however, they were used as struts to support—or, rather, to suspend in mid-air—a mammoth cylinder some sixty feet long. (The downward distance from this same point is ninety feet.) The cylinder, which is the part that is called the Lantern, was then filled with glass, trimmed with carved wood, and covered on the outside with stone, and when done threw a load of four hundred tons on the eight pillars of the Octagon. So well did the medieval craftsmen figure their stresses that for some six hundred years now the Lantern has fulfilled its purpose —to concentrate a flood of light directly in front of the choir, and thus to bathe the entry of the cathedral's most sanctified spot in heavenly radiance.

'One thing I *do* know about this cathdral,' Mrs Severs said, 'is that there's a famous Victorian monument somewhere around. Or perhaps "notorious" would be a better word.'

We found it, in close juxtaposition to the splendid Norman south door of the church, and somehow the thought struck me that the two sets of people—the robust Victorians, and the men of the Middle Ages who cut those twisted pillars and gave them their bold carvings—would have had a lot in common.

The 'monument' is a tombstone erected in 1845 to the memory of William Pickering and Richard Edger, who apparently were killed (on the day before Christmas) when working on the rail-road that was then being built to Ely. The tombstone bears this verse:

The Spiritual Railway
The line to heaven by Christ was made,
With heavenly truth the Rails are laid,
From Earth to Heaven the Line extends

To Life Eternal where it ends.
Repentance is the Station then
Where Passengers are taken in.
No Fee for them is there to pay
For Jesus is himself the way.
God's Word is the first Engineer
It points the way to Heaven so clear.
Through tunnels dark and dreary here
It does the way to Glory steer.
God's Love the Fire, his Truth the Steam,
Which drives the Engine and the Train.
All you who would to Glory ride,
Must come to Christ, in him abide.
In First and Second and Third Class,
Repentance, Faith and Holiness,
You must the way to Glory gain
Or you with Christ will not remain.
Come then poor Sinners, now's the time
At any Station on the Line.
If you'll repent and turn from sin
The Train will stop and take you in.

On starting back to Oxford, George stopped for gas at a service station on the outskirts of Cambridge. Nearby was a little sweet-shop, and outside on the pavement stood a metal sign advertising 7-Up. 'I'll be darned,' I said, 'I thought Coca-Cola had Great Britain all sewed up. For old times' sake, let's have one.'

The rosy-faced young woman who uncapped the unchilled bottles for us was disposed to pass the time of day. We agreed that the spring had been lovely, although a mite dry. She asked what part of the States we came from; we said, 'California'; and *she* said, 'Think of that!' She asked us how we were liking England, and we said we liked it fine. She said, 'You *do*?'—with that overtone of surprise, followed by pleasure, that we had so often encountered already in England. Apparently Americans are supposed to complain about something.

Then we told her that we'd been visiting the university. 'Very grand it is,' she said without noticeable warmth, 'and now, of course, you'll be going to the American cemetery. A lovely place. My husband and I did our courting there.'

George and I had no intention of visiting the American cemetery, which we had noticed on the way into Cambridge, but now our interest was piqued. It's off the road a bit, but almost as soon as one drives into the grounds one can see Old Glory on a flagpole up ahead.

Cambridge's is one of several American military cemeteries in Europe. The War Graves Commission deserves the highest praise for it. One might claim with justice that the chapel is too high for its width, or that the sculptures of American fighting men, posted like sentries along a long wall, are a shade too big for their setting. But the over-all effect is dignified and serene. A series of pools edged with rosebushes makes a kind of mall from the entrance to the chapel, and all the plantings are well kept. The graves lie on a broad, flat sweep of velvety grass, row after row of neat white crosses, with here and there a Star of David as a grace note. Beyond and below them, to a far horizon, stretches a broad expanse of English countryside, a restful symphony of rolling hills and little valleys. And over all arches the cloud-swept sky, the beautiful, boundless English sky.

It should be a source of pride and a comfort to the wives or mothers of those men who lie buried in this spot that it is so lovely that English couples do their courting there.

By the middle of June the myriad greens of spring had gone, and only the burnished oxblood of the copper beeches relieved the velvety dark greenness of the tree tops.

The roses came resoundingly into bloom—scarlet, crimson, apricot, ivory, pink, and gold—against a cool backdrop of delphiniums. Out in the country the verges of the roads were gay with red and rose and pale pink poppies, their fragile petals quivering with every puff of wind.

Gardeners had long since looped the jonquil leaves into tidy knots and had lifted the early radishes from the cold frames; now gardens (and shops) were burgeoning with spring onions, leaf lettuce, succulent baby beans, and tender young rhubarb. Our bushes yielded a seemingly endless bounty of raspberries, meltingly sweet; these, and the new potatoes we dug just before cooking them, made each meal a gastronomic delight.

In June, too, the first salmon came into market. Paler and more delicate in flavour than the Chinook salmon we know on the west coast of America, it turned us into gluttons. English housewives gently cook the whole fish in bouillon and serve it cold, often with crisp cucumbers, and achieve a dish that is ambrosial.

Brussels sprouts were *out* of season.

Surprisingly—it rains all the time in England, ask any American—late June also ushered in a spell of drought. The once-glossy foliage of trees and bushes acquired a dusty film, lawns burned to yellow, and vegetables drooped in dried-out soil. Hardly any householder was equipped to withstand drought; in fact, those few who watered their lawns or gardens with hoses and sprinklers severely taxed the water supply of Oxford, and had to be asked to restrict their usage.

The air hummed with the traffic of bees and wasps. The latter invaded bakeries and fruit stalls, household marmalade jars and fruit bowls, their access simplified by the open windows and doors that the English prefer to effete American screens. 'Mrs Blount, I don't care if we stifle to death in here, I will *not* have wasps in my house!' I kept saying. Mrs Blount would shake her head. It was bad enough that I insisted on drying our woollies indoors, without benefit of good English air, but to keep the windows closed in weather as fine as this. . . .

Finally, with a crash and a bang, the granddaddy of all electrical storms dumped a cloudburst and three weeks of showers on us; and England was green again.

Days had grown long. In May you could read a newpaper outdoors at nine, and then at ten in the evening, and by mid-June the sunset glow was lingering, silvery pink in the sky, until almost eleven at night. (No contrast was greater, on returning to California, than to have night fall as if someone had suddenly turned off the lights in a ballroom.) It was a time for seeing Greek plays at twilight in college gardens, for having tea on terraces, for idling through the woods or along the water walks; in short, for taking life easy.

Only the young were tense. Red was staying up until all hours cramming for the exams his housemaster had thought it would be sporting for him to take. These were called O-levels; 'O' stands for 'Ordinary'. Had he been an English schoolboy, he would have taken them in the following year, eight of them instead of the three he was tackling now. They were a necessary preamble to having a shot at the A (for Advanced) levels, at age seventeen or eighteen, which qualify a student for university admission.

At the top of the educational ladder, at the university itself, the Honour Schools were in session. Americans would say that 'finals' were in progress. For some thirty-six hours of writing, undergraduates were pouring out what they'd learned in their three or four years of tutorials and reading; and the gutters outside the examination building on the High were nightly yielding a rich harvest of champagne corks. Friends who were currently being spared the woe that was going on inside the building would wait outside on the steps; and when the drained-dry undergraduates came shuffling out after writing their last paper, there would be a bottle of champagne awaiting them. To be drunk on the spot.

But for the rest of us, it was a relaxed time, a sit-back-in-your-chair-and-chat time. Lifting his brandy and sighting into its amber depths, someone at a dinner party would begin, 'It seems to me the undergraduates are growing rather bolder in the matter of boutonnieres. Carnations weren't so bad . . . but *irises!*'

And then, to us, 'They've got to wear proper *subfusc*, not even coloured stockings, you know, for Schools. The carnation boutonniere is a sort of harmless protest. Expression of independence, and all that. But *irises!*'

Someone else would chime in. 'D'you think there's any truth to that tale about the tankard of ale?' Another voice would say, 'No matter. As long as it makes a good story, Oxford likes it. Tell the Beadles.'

'All right. It goes this way. An undergraduate is said to have come to Schools armed with a secret weapon from the Statutes. . . .'

Interruption from the chair in the shadow across the room. 'Ridiculous to think himself more clever than the dons, what?'

'. . . and after he'd sat himself down, he demanded that the invigilator fetch him the tankard of ale to which the Statutes entitle him.'

From the chair in shadow: 'Rather clever of him at that, though.'

'So the invigilator *did* fetch the ale. And then sent him out of the hall. Told him he couldn't return until he was wearing his sword. The Statutes require *that*, too.'

General laughter. Puffing of pipes in a moment of serene

silence. Then a new conversational tangent. 'According to gossip . . .' someone would begin.

'Which is undoubtedly Oxford's second most durable commodity, ranking just after motor-cars and just before marmalade.' another voice would cut in.

'According to gossip, there were twenty-six thousand volumes of books in Canon Jenkins' lodgings, and no nightwear.'

Someone would chuckle. 'Do you recall the notice he once had inserted in the *Gazette,* offering to supply "informal instruction and miracles"?'

'And his blazing pipes?' someone else would say. 'Sometimes they shot blue flames. I was told that he carried his sleeping pills in his tobacco pouch, and occasionally tamped a few into his pipe along with the tobacco.'

Canon Jenkins had died, at eighty-plus, shortly after we had come to Oxford. 'He was unmarried,' his obituary in *The Times* had concluded, 'having an equal aversion to women and to cats.' A much-loved old gentleman, his longer-lasting obituary was the fond regard of people who had known him; and these recollections in turn would lead to anecdotes about other Oxford eccentrics, a long and honourable line.

The Heads of colleges, especially in the nineteenth century, were a notable lot. They ranged in temperament all the way from the strong-willed Lindsay of Balliol to gentle Spooner of New College—Spooner of the twisted tongue, whose name lives on in spoonerism. Lindsay knew what he wanted, and usually got it. Once the Fellows turned down a proposal he favoured, voting 8-1 against him. 'Well, gentlemen,' he said. 'We seem to have reached an impasse'—and adjourned the meeting. Spooner, who couldn't have uttered half the spoonerisms attributed to him, probably *did* say, when advising an undergraduate to get a bicycle, 'Young man, what you need in Oxford is a well-boiled icicle.' And he *did* announce in college chapel that the congregation would now sing the hymn that begins with 'conquering kings'—only Spooner switched it to 'kinkering kongs'. But it's probably libelous to credit him with a transposition of the 'b' and 'h' upon intending to remark that he liked nothing better than a fine boar's head on a cold winter night.

By June our university acquaintances had learned that we didn't react to critical comment about the United States as if the speaker were attacking motherhood and the Flag, and they began to swap anecdotes with us.

One evening we had been talking about national stereotypes, and I was telling a group about an experience of a friend of mine. She and her husband had saved for years in order to finance the trip and their sabbatical stay in England, and they had nothing left over for luxuries. 'So you can imagine their pleasure,' I said, 'when they were invited to a grand orders-and-decorations banquet at the Dorchester. The only flaw in my friend's pleasure was that she had no evening wrap—just an old cloth coat.

'Fortunately, the people with whom they were going to the banquet were not only rich but approachable, so my friend asked her hostess if she happened to have an extra wrap of some sort; and she was given her choice of two, both fur. On the night of the banquet, as the women were queued up to leave off their wraps, my friend noticed that another pair of guests were watching her intently as well as listening to her conversation with her hostess. And as she turned away to go to the banquet hall, she heard one of them say, "Did you notice her fur? These rich Americans have everything!" '

Mrs. Evans-Hume chuckled. 'That reminds me of how excited I was when we learned we were to have a year at Princeton. I could hardly wait to do my cooking in one of those splendid American kitchens full of appliances that do all the work while one stands off to the side and tends the buttons. But the house that was let for us there wasn't as up-to-date as mine here in Oxford.'

'I had a fine kitchen, when we were in the States,' Mary Rowlands said, 'especially the fridge. I remember how thrilling it was, the day we arrived, to find that some thoughtful faculty lady had completely stocked it with food for us. This is an example of that wonderful American hospitality, I thought. Especially when I found a note, which had been slipped under the butter dish, on which there was a schedule of dates and the names of the ladies who would be coming to call on those days. I was so pleased, and I told Henry, "Isn't that American efficiency, though?" ' She giggled. 'And then not one of the ladies ever showed up.'

I drew my breath. 'Oh, Mary,' I said. 'I think that's shocking.'

'They were terribly nice later,' she said. 'And we ended by

having a most enjoyable stay. I must say I rather miss those supermarkets.'

'They're coming, though,' another lady remarked. 'The self-service stores are enormously successful. One can hardly get through the aisles.'

'And the variety of frozen food increases all the time,' someone else said. 'There's nothing especially novel any more about pre-sliced and packaged bread, and I've noted that the Co-ops are pre-cutting their meat and putting it in plastic film, as is done in the States.'

'The one near me on the London Road has installed a rotissomat,' I remarked. 'They're cooking young broilers on spits under infra-red heat, and selling the whole bird for ten bob.'

'But the innovations that are a great success in America don't always catch on here,' Mrs Evans-Hume said. 'Remember when cake mixes were introduced? In the early fifties, wasn't it? In America one sees dozens of different kinds, but I believe there are only one or two that have survived in England. And putting tea into paper packets has been a failure here too.'

I disputed that. 'I'm not sure tea bags have been such a failure,' I said. 'There are three different brands on display at the shop where I trade. Any time there's enough business to support three brands of anything, *somebody* buys it. I don't suppose any of you . . . ?'

They all looked shocked, and shook their heads.

While we had been making these comparisons, I'd been tempted to say that Britain is beginning to catch up with the United States in supplying well-designed, tasteful clothing and household goods for the masses, but I refrained. Imagine claiming that my young, raw country has better taste than the country that produced Wedgwood and Chippendale, Wren and Adam! But, of course, that's what has happened in the course of the past thirty years. The great levelling of society that has taken place in the United States has upgraded the taste of the middle and lower classes, who now buy good copies of Swedish modern instead of massive two-colour mohair 'suites'; who are less frightened of abstract art and symphony orchestras than they used to be; and who have learned to prize simplicity in both dress and interior decoration. (A comparison of the modern Sears Roebuck catalogue with one published in the 1930s will prove the point.) Increasing knowledgeability and sophistication in popular taste are coming to England now—with such shrewd merchandisers as Marks and Spencer (a British equivalent of Penney's) and the mass-circulation women's magazines leading the way. But there is still an enormous gulf in England between the taste of the classes and the masses.

Meanwhile, over on the men's side of the room, George was saying, '. . . and of course if the chap hadn't had so much wine, he would never have been so outspoken. Apparently, they'd been informally "dedicating" the lab all afternoon. I'd given my speech at four, not a very good one, I'm afraid; and then there'd been the official dedication, with quantities of sherry afterward. Finally, this young fellow—a pretty recent graduate, I'd say— came up to me, and grabbed the lapels of my suit jacket. . . .'

The men around George smiled. The fellow must have been quite drunk. Englishmen normally avoid all personal contact. They don't grab lapels to command attention; they clear their throats or point their pipes at each other.

'. . . and then he said, "Professor Beadle, that was a most enlightening lecture. Far better, if I may say so, than the series you gave at University College, London. Much less turgid." '

George's Oxford audience laughed heartily. For a young graduate to speak so candidly to a professor meant that he had been *very* drunk.

'That's the only time since we've been in England that I've known for sure what someone thought of my efforts,' George concluded. 'In fact, I could have done with some of that out-spokenness during my first series of lectures here. I'd stop every fifteen minutes and ask if anyone had questions, and nobody ever peeped a peep. Then, afterwards, when the hall had nearly emptied, someone would come up and ask a question that indicated I'd probably snowed the lot of them. Talked over their heads, I mean. It was very frustrating.'

John Cavendish spoke up. 'I had the same experience in reverse, when I did that year at Dartmouth. It was shattering to be halted during a lecture and asked to do a better job of it. Not that they put it quite that way. It was on the order of, "Come again, Professor, if you don't mind?"'

'Of course, I *did* mind, because the object of lecturing at Oxford isn't to instruct the young, but rather to show off one's own bag of tricks, and I considered the undergraduates at Dartmouth most impertinent. . . . They were really just frightfully keen, and nobody has ever told them that children should be seen and not heard. In the end, I came rather to like their insistence on getting the facts. Keeps one on one's toes.'

'It's interesting,' George said, 'how the English and American schools operate in reverse. We give our youngsters much more freedom in secondary school than you do, but tighten the reins considerably when they go to college—more required courses, more frequent exams, lots more pressure all around. You give them no freedom to speak of until they get to university, and then you turn them completely loose.'

A schoolmaster in the group —he'd just returned from an exchange year at a New York boys' school—said, 'Perhaps that's because America keeps all its youth, including the dull ones, in school until they are eighteen? And because you don't apply selective procedures until they reach university age? I should hazard a guess, in fact, that you use the university *itself* as your selective device. Something on the order of half your youth now go to "college", I believe? Here, it's far less, as you know. At my school, only 11 per cent prepare for university—so, of course, we have to wind them up sooner.'

'It's too bad they have to specialize so early. Yours,' George said. 'I don't know how it is in the humanities, but in the sciences a good many undergraduates here are weak outside their areas of specialty. One of the boys I've been tutoring, a very bright young fellow, has got interested in virology and would like to do his doctoral research at Caltech. But he's been trained as a classical botanist, and his background in maths and physics is hopelessly inadequate. The only way we can take him at Caltech is to admit him on condition that he go back to school first and learn some calculus.'

'Go back to school? An *Oxford* graduate?' (This from a nonscientist don.)

'I'm afraid so,' George replied. 'I must say it's been a surprise to me to find that some undergraduates here haven't been as well prepared by their secondary schools, particularly in maths, as many of those who come into Caltech from American comprehensive high schools.'

A chill suddenly descended; it was that word 'comprehensive' that had done it. So George moved rapidly to dispel it. 'Of course, I'm talking about only a limited number,' he said. 'Those few who've grown interested in one of the areas in modern science which have become a synthesis of several specialties. Biochemical genetics, for example, is a blending of chemistry, physics, and biology, with maths as the foundation. . . . Incidentally, Mr Cavendish, how did you like having all your Dartmouth boys present at *every* lecture, writing down every word you spoke?'

The tension eased in a general laugh, for Oxford undergraduates aren't the inveterate lecture-goers and note-takers that American college students are. With good reason. Nobody is going to examine them on the content of any course—only on their over-all knowledge, when it comes time for Honour Schools. Which reminded someone else of a good story:

'Reynolds was telling me last week of how he averted a crisis in our relations with Latin America. Seems he had a man from Argentina—or perhaps it was Bolivia—anyway, he was scheduled to give a lecture that afternoon, and you know how fine the weather has been. Reynolds realized that the undergraduates would in all likelihood be punting on the river. But he also realized that the gentleman from Argentina—or Bolivia, or wherever it was—would consider an empty lecture hall as a personal insult.

'So Reynolds persuaded some of the staff and their wives to come by, and he telephoned a general invitation to the finishing schools roundabout—they're *full* of girls from South America, you know—and the fortunate result was that the assigned lecture room was found to be too small. The entire crowd had to move to a larger one, and the V.I.P. was very flattered. But Reynolds had been quite right in his initial assumption. The undergraduates were on the river.'

The river was a good place to be on a warm June afternoon. The Thames Valley is cut by hundreds of streams, none of them deep or fast-flowing; and it was a never-ending source of delight to me—who have never, in my citified life, even *seen* an ole swimmin' hole—to watch people sunning themselves on grassy riverbanks or diving from half-submerged tree trunks into the green-brown water.

Southern California children know nothing but tiled pools

and seashore sand, and Red reacted with horror to the idea of
putting his bare feet into *mud*. But he learned to paddle a kayak.
He and his friend Francis Cooke spent one exhilarating Sunday
afternoon swooping and turning—like terriers yapping at a St
Bernard—around the punt that George, with grunts and
occasional profanity, was learning to pole. It looks so easy when
an experienced punter goes gliding past, but the tyro must guard
both against pushing with uneven force (which makes the boat
veer) and thrusting his pole too deeply into the river bed (which
can result in his being left dangling on the pole while the punt
shoots out from under him).

One Sunday we took an all-day boat trip on the Thames. It
was a bittersweet day. Lovely in its beginnings, with the brilliantly colourful, tidy gardens of the lockkeepers and the stately
processes of opening and closing locks as counterpoint to the
intervening green and quiet stretches of the river. The one flaw
was that volume of traffic (a variable, of course, according to
weather) affects the speed with which craft can pass through
the locks— and our steamer spent so much time in watery queues
that we didn't get to Marlow, the end of the run, until three in
the afternoon, two hours behind schedule.

Stupidly, we had brought no lunch; nothing but orange squash
had been sold aboard; and watching our more foresighted fellow
passengers dig into their picnic hampers had further whetted our
appetites. The boat would return, on schedule, thirty minutes
hence—so, the minute it tied up at Marlow, we thundered down
the landing stage in search of food. 'Now, if you'll take whatever
is ready and don't ask for anything special, we might have time
for a whole meal,' George warned, as he paced us through a park
and up to the town.

One café was open. We studied the menu, making our choices
on the basis of what would be quick. Then the manager
approached us. He was most regretful. He had run out of food.
'The boat is nearly always late,' he reflected sadly and sym-
pathetically, 'and Sunday after Sunday, there are people like
yourselves whom I must disappoint.'

We lunched on ice-cream bars, snatched at a stand in the park
as the boat cast off for the return trip. George was as close to a
black fury as he ever gets, and spent the journey back hatching
schemes for making pots of money out of opportunities the Eng-

lish ignore. The first of these schemes involved selling box
lunches on the landing stage at Marlow.

'I just don't understand the English lack of enterprise,' he said.
'Look at Oxford. *One* Wimpy's. *One* Palm's. Why isn't anybody
smart enough to imitate them?'

Wimpy's is a hamburger joint in the civic centre; always
jammed, and not just with Americans. Mrs Palm's is the
delicatessen that is the foreigners' home-away-from-home in
Oxford, the only place where one can get rye bread and chili
powder and avocados and spicy German sausage. She did a
land-office business. And as George said, neither place had any
competition.

'Add launderettes to your list,' I said. 'I've started going again
to the one on the London Road. With so little rain, our stuff has
a pretty good chance of drying outdoors now.

'Well, the manager told me she'd missed seeing me, and I said
I'd have been a regular customer all along if she'd had hot-air
dryers. She said, "Yes, many American ladies have praised the
convenience of such dryers." But she was only being polite; you
know, as if I'd just told her how deep the Grand Canyon is. Then
she went on to say that *English* ladies prefer their laundry ready
for the iron.

'I'd like to test that. So, after you've made your first profits on
selling box lunches at Marlow, *I'm* going to install hot-air dryers
in a launderette somewhere. I have a feeling that English ladies
might be good and ready to forgo the pleasures of wrestling
damp bed sheets back and forth across their ironing boards.'

'Yes, but Mom'—Red insists on being fair, which is a great
inconvenience on occasions like this one—'you've been saying all
along how nice it's been to get away from American standardization and efficiency. You've been saying how much you like the
slower pace here, and that there's no high-pressure selling, and
that everything is more personal than at home.'

It was a good point. I *did* like the lack of rush. The English
don't look or act as harried as Americans. They don't frown as
often, and smile more. The English storekeeper takes the time
to say, 'Good morning' before he asks if he may serve you; the
American says, 'What'll it be for you?' with preamble, or just,
'Who's next?'

I also like the flexibility of most English rules. Imagine any

American librarian refusing to collect the fine on a book because
it was 'only one day past due.' It had been entertaining to
observe that temporary 'No Parking' signs got shifted about
quite openly by motorists hungry for parking places; and we
never met a pubkeeper or wine merchant in England who refused
to sell us cider or spirits a little before or a little after 'hours'.

I was enormously impressed, too, by the English system of
magistrates, in which all breaches of the peace are first heard in
a neighbourhood court by a citizen-judge—someone appointed
to the job because of intelligence and background, not because he
or she possesses special expertise. The magistrate is free to dispose
of those cases that need go to no higher court in most any way
that seems sensible. (A legal adviser sits with the magistrate, but
only to see that his disposition of the case doesn't *break* the law.)
In America such a system would be too casual and would soon
be codified, the magistrate either being forced to stand for
election or to qualify as an expert under Ordinance No. 1783,
Section 2.45, Subsection (c) of some municipal code.

Musing on in this vein, as the launch cut slowly through the
quiet waters of the Thames, I said to George, 'Red's right, you
know. Even if it isn't very fast or efficient, there's a lot to be
said for muddling through. Think of the affair of the crossed
cheque. At home, you'd still be waiting for your money.'

George smiled. 'That *was* a funny one, wasn't it?'

As a protective device, most English cheques either come with
two lines printed vertically across the face or the person who
draws the cheque pens in two comparable lines. This 'crossing'
prevents the cheque's being cashed; it must be deposited, first,
to the account of the person or firm to whom it is drawn. As for
accounts, there are two kinds: internal and external. Ours was
the latter; they exist for the convenience of foreigners like ourselves, who had brought dollars into Britain. (They make possible
one's taking home an equivalent sum.) British law forbids the
deposit of sterling into an external account—unless the person
or institution issuing the cheque has been authorised to do so.
Oxford *had* been, and the pounds put into our account were what
fed us. But other British institutions did not, naturally, have the
proper authorization, since George came to them—to give a
lecture, for example—only as a transient visitor.

The 'affair of the crossed cheque' had come about this way:

George had conducted a seminar at a Scottish university, and had been reimbursed by cheque for his travel expenses. When he got back to Oxford and took it into the bank, he discovered that it was a crossed cheque. So he couldn't cash it. But he couldn't deposit it, either, because its deposit into an external account hadn't been authorized.

He and the bank clerk had stood looking at the cheque as it lay on the counter between them. It appeared to be no good to either of them.

'Well,' George had finally remarked, 'what'll we do with it?'

'Allow me to confer with the manager, sir,' the clerk had said.

The manager had joined the two of them at the window. There had been the ghost of a smile on his lips.

'You'd be spending this money here in England, wouldn't you, sir?' he'd asked.

'Sure would,' George had replied.

'Then . . . ah . . . perhaps the best solution to the problem might be to cash it for you?'

'That strikes me as an . . . ah . . . *admirable* solution,' George had said, adopting a favourite English adjective for a uniquely English situation.

We *had* spent it, too. Right down the street, at Shergold's, for paraffin.

Still to come was our last day in Oxford, when we bundled our dirty clothes and other leftovers into two packages and took them to the Headington Post Office. One weighed 9½ lbs. and was speedily dispatched. But the other at 11 lbs. 1 oz., was just an ounce too heavy to qualify for the 8- to 11-lb. parcel-post rate. The clerk's face puckered into a familiar expression, and we knew what was coming. Whenever a package *barely* weighed into a given rate block—this one was just into the 11- to 15-lb. rate—the girls at the post office tried to persuade the customer to take the package home and re-wrap it. (We never wanted to, and always did, not daring to behave like wasteful Americans in the face of that frugal British concern for our pocketbooks.)

On this particular day, however, the clerk happened to look at us before she voiced the customary suggestion. We'd been packing and house-cleaning for a week and it was obvious now, from our weary faces, that we were bone-tired. So, instead of advising us to take the package home, she looked George directly in the eye, and said, firmly, 'I make it just on the line at eleven pounds, sir.'

Wonderful people.

I'd still like to give those box lunches and hot-air dryers a try, though.

Chapter 12

WE'D BEEN in queue outside the Sheldonian Theatre for twenty minutes, Red and I, and my fashionably pointed shoes were starting to pinch. So I leaned back against the iron railings of the fence—just a little, not enough to risk dirtying my best print dress or my long white doeskin gloves. Red was wearing his best too: grey flannel suit (the trousers a bit high over the ankles now), the silk version of his school tie around his neck, and his pristine straw boater, its band in school colours, set square on his head.

'Pop will be having his second glass of champagne about now,' I said. 'Pretty high living, eh? Champagne and strawberries at eleven in the morning. Courtesy of the Right Honourable Nathaniel Lord Crewe, Bishop of Durham, dead these more than two hundred years.'

'Oh,' said Red. 'The Creweian Benefaction! You mean he left the money for *strawberries and champagne?*'

'Sure did. A whole five pounds per annum. That was probably a lot of money in the eighteenth century. But I doubt it even begins to pay for the refreshments that the bigwigs are lapping up over at Magdalen today.'

The cheering cup of wine was a good idea for someone like George, since it would make his processional march through the streets of Oxford, in full academic regalia, a little more endurable. That's what I was thinking as our queue outside the Sheldonian started to move; actually, as I realized when I set eyes on him thirty minutes later, I needn't have worried about his discomfort in the spotlight. He'd been with Dame* Margot Fonteyn the whole while, and he bounced into the Sheldonian looking as buoyant as if he'd just been elected president of her fan club.

---

* Americans tend to choke a little when they say this title, doubtless because they've heard so often that there's nothing like a dame. A Dame, however, is a lady who's been knighted. She can't be a Lady because a Lady is the lady of a *man* who's been knighted.

The reason that George was eating strawberries and drinking champagne, and the reason that Red and I were queued up for seats at the Sheldonian, was that today was Oxford's Encaenia—the fanciest university ceremonial of the year, when honorary degrees are awarded. George was to get one. So was Dame Margot. And five others: Prime Minister Robert Menzies of Australia; Sir William Penney (head of Britain's atomic weapons research); Lord Somerville of Harrow (a lord of appeal, equivalent to a justice of the U.S. Supreme Court); historian Peter Geyl; and German scholar Eliza Butler.

Red and I were to sit above them, somewhere on the benches that ring the circular theatre. The honorands were to stand in the pit, holding onto their poise as best they could, while hundreds of eyes focused on them, and the Public Orator extolled their virtues in a language that none of them understood. Even their names would be Latinized. Then the Chancellor would shake their hands and admit them to the rights and privileges of their new degrees.

Of the seven, Dame Margot and Prime Minister Menzies were the two in whom the public was most interested. A few years back, when Harry Truman had received a honorary degree at a ceremony like this, the undergraduates had lined the parade route up to the Sheldonian, yelling 'Give 'em hell, Harricum!' But the American honorand at *this* June's Encaenia lacked Harricum's high position or fame and was just the guy lucky enough to have drawn the beautiful ballerina as his partner in the procession. ('Luck, nothing!' George says. 'It was fast footwork.') It was she around whom the photographers swarmed.

The procession had started marching across town from Magdalen at just about the time we took our seats in the Sheldonian. I should have liked to see them, but had no fault to find with the spectacle in Technicolor and Vista Vision that was unfolding where I was. The dons were assembling. There was a bustle of activity on the floor, a shimmer of white shirt fronts and bow ties, a constant shifting of colour as their hoods swung toward the viewer, or away: the lot of them looked like a cage full of parakeets.

At noon precisely they stopped twittering. The galleries hushed. The organist played the final chord of a Bach fugue. And we all sat silent, waiting.

Then the great centre doors swung open. Outside, in the bright sunlight, we could see a blaze of scarlet and blue and a glint of gold. The procession marched in—not very smartly, but with the dignity of the ages. First, the university marshal and the verger. Then the mace-bearing beadles. Then the Chancellor: Lord Halifax, nearing eighty now, and bent beneath the weight of his years and his robe of office. (He died the following year.) He was wearing court dress, with black satin breeches, and a black brocaded gown with sleeves and hem encrusted with gold lace. An undergraduate page carried his train. Behind him came the Vice-Chancellor and the proctors, the snowy ecclesiastical 'bands' under their chins starched to highest Puritan standards. Then the Heads of House and other university officials. Finally the Doctors. Divinity, medicine, music, letters, science, civil law. They sat in two crimson lines on either side of the Chancellor's throne.

We sang 'God Save the Queen.'

The Chancellor declared the Convocation open. ('What funny-sounding Latin,' I whispered to Red. 'Old-style pronunciation,' he whispered back.)

The beadles went out returning with a bunched-up band of honorands; now there was a Beadle in the pit, too. They all sat demurely, on opposite sides of the little aisle, like children at dancing school.

First up was Menzies—a tall man, straight and vigorous, with a face that made one feel good just to look at it, and eyebrows like circumflexes. A ripple of laughter coursed through the Sheldonian when the Public Orator said something about '*Matildam ad chorum invitatum.*' One doesn't have to be stuffy, just because one is speaking Latin, and apparently he had just alleged that the Prime Minister likes to explore the Australian outback while singing 'Waltzing Matilda'.

Menzies got a bigger hand than those lesser-known personages who followed him—Donaldum Baronem Somervell de Herga, Elizam Marian Butler, and Petrum Geyl—but the star of the show was clearly Dominam Margot Fonteyn de Arias. She was getting an honorary doctorate of music, a degree whose gown is a creamy brocade with facings of shocking-pink silk. It is a robe enormously becoming to a woman, and her skin was very nearly the same ivory as the brocade. Her carriage was superb, of course,

and the fine black silk jersey dress and double strand of pearls
one could glimpse when she moved did nothing to destroy the
illusion of grace and elegance she projects from the stage. She
was doubly in the news at that particular time because her
Panamanian diplomat husband had just been involved in an
abortive revolution. Hence, when she rose to stand beside the
Public Orator, the entire audience in the Sheldonian—as one
person and with one rustle—leaned forward to get a good look.
Had I been in her place, I should have felt like the last pickle
in the jar, with tongs coming at me. She just lifted her chin a
little, and smiled.

The Public Orator let her off easy—no jokes, just some flowery
references to the fact that her 'shapely physique is transfigured
by genius.' Or, at least, that's how the official translation of
'corpori venusto addit ingeni dotes' read. Obviously a bachelor
don—an old bachelor don—had done the translation.

Willelmus Georgius Penney came next; and then Georgium
Wells Beadle. The Public Orator had had a flash of inspiration
when he had been considering how to describe George's work
with bread mould: 'Legimus in libro Iosue e Gabaonitis dissimu-
landi causa ostentatos esse panes mucore corruptos,' he began,
and everyone smiled. How clever of him to have remembered
the reference in the Book of Joshua to the Gibeonites having
'used mouldy loaves to further their deceit.' The Public Orator
made it clear, however, that George had been interested in
furthering scientific truth, using 'fungum illium qui appelatur
Neurospora crassa.' George got a big grin on his face at that
point, partly because it was comforting to recognize the familiar
botanical name, and partly because it sounded so odd to hear
Neurospora crassa restored to the company of its kinfolk in an
entire Latin sentence. And he looked impressed, in spite of himself, when the Public Orator got to the grand finale; Latin
does have a majestic rhythm to it: 'Presento vobis hospitem
acceptissimum Georgium Wells Beadle, Artium Magistratum,
Collegio de Balliolo ascriptum, Praemio Nobeliano donatum, ut
admittatur honoris causa ad gradum Doctoris in Scientia.'

The rest of the Encaenia programme included recitations—
from high pulpits hung midway between the galleries and the
pit—by undergraduates who had won prizes for their various
compositions. Miss Stephanie Roberta Pickard of Somerville

read a bit of her translation into Greek of a *Circassian Love Chaunt* by Coleridge; Mr David Patrick Walley of Merton quoted a few verses from his Latin poem on space travel; and a Balliol man with a Scots burr and the lovely name of James Iain Wilson Brash gave us an inkling of Gladstone's views on education.

Finally, the spotlight swung back to the Public Orator, whose Creweian Oration was similar to an annual report. This time there were English translations in our hands, so *everyone* could appreciate the wit and wisdom of the speaker. His best laugh came when, in referring to that spring's great Latin debate, he recommended that the opposing factions take Vergil's advice: '*Claudite iam rivos, pueri, sat prata biberunt*' ('Dry up, my lads, the meadows are awash'). Finally he came to a graceful conclusion, and in the same sentence suggested that it was time for lunch. Then the Chancellor dissolved the Convocation, and off we all went.

University officials, the honorands, and other distinguished guests were to have lunch at All Souls College. So I sent Red off to whatever culinary treat the cooks at the Muni had prepared that day for their schoolboy trade, and followed in the wake of the official procession to All Souls. When I finally found George, in the quadrangle under the great Wren sundial, he was just relinquishing Dame Margot to the Vice-Chancellor. He acknowledged my congratulations on his honour with a far more gracious and benevolent smile than husbands customarily bestow on wives. Dame Margot—and I mean no disrespect—must be quite a dame.

Among the notables who needed no introduction was Sir Anthony Eden, an elegant sight in his scarlet D.C.L. robe with squashy velvet bonnet. There, too, was Sir Alan Herbert, the lawyer-author whose *Holy Deadlock* played a major part in getting the English divorce laws modified. At the moment we strolled past him, he and Lord Halifax had their academic headgear point to point, and Sir Alan was saying, 'Now, just the other day I was telling Winston . . .'

We lingered within earshot while Professor Geyl, a Dutchman, finished the anecdote he was telling the Master of Balliol and Lady Keir. 'It *is* a difficult name for the English to pronounce,' he was saying, ' So I have become quite accustomed to being called "Guile". Except at any London club, of course. There, the porters mark my messages, "For Mr G-a-l-e".' George and I smiled, too, and walked on. A very English story. The porters would be Cockneys; and 'Guile' would be the Cockney pronunciation of a surname written 'Gale'.

The Mayor of Oxford was at the luncheon party too, his gold chain of office in a wide loop about his shoulders. The Dean of Christ Church, sweating a bit under his clerical collar and his heavy robe of red wool and black velvet, was talking to the Mayoress. (That's the mayor's wife. Once in a while, the mayor is a woman. But she is still addressed as 'Mr Mayor'. And I suppose that her husband, poor thing, is the mayoress.) The Heads of House and the Doctors made a gaudy splash of colour against the old stone walls of the college. By comparison the women at the party looked like wrens. The feminine honours seemed to be about equally divided between Dame Margot and the Right Honourable Robert Gordon Menzies' trim little Dame Patty.

We lunched in the library—a vast, two-storied room, its proportions and architectural detail an example of the eighteenth century at its elegant best. A priceless collection of rare books is housed there, behind beautiful brass grilles. We ate turbot in shrimp sauce. Jellied chicken and asparagus. Coffee ice cream with overtones of rum. Strawberries as big as plums, with cream almost too heavy to pour. And coffee, afterwards, in the quadrangle.

'You could certainly get used to this life, couldn't you?' George said when he finally found me. I was leaning up against a doorway, sipping coffee, and blissfully watching all the pretty people.

They began to drift away by three. We went over to Balliol, to allow George to remove—for a bit—his weighty scarlet robe. Then we set out again; this time for the Vice-Chancellor's Garden Party, the university's 'family party' of the year. (Gowns are worn but wives are brought.) George and I sat on a low wall and watched them arrive: it's a splendid show, in case prospective tourists who are reading this can arrange to be in the vicinity of the Vice-Chancellor's college at 4 p.m. on the Wednesday of the week following Trinity Full Term, and the weather's fine.

Behind those college gates, on this particular Wednesday of the week following Trinity Full Term, the dons wandered about sipping tea and admiring the plantings in the Magdalen College gardens, making mental notes that the gardeners at their own colleges ought to be gingered up a bit. The dons' wives wandered about sipping tea and appraising each other's hats; for an organdy mobcap of the type Mrs Smathers has got, one *does* need a well-defined chin line, doesn't one? There was chitchat about the O.U.D.S. production of *The Birds*; and how nice it was to have all the examinations done with, only the *vivas* left; and what plans have you made for the Long Vac? Nobody asked us if we were missing our steam heating, or if we were getting to see any of the *real* England. I was both elated and depressed. 'George,' I said, 'we've finally made it. We're members of the family. And in just three weeks we've got to go home!'

We wandered down to that part of the garden that is bisected by a bit of the river. In the beds along the gravelled paths the Canterbury bells were standing as tall and proud as any Head of House, the larkspur hazy blue beside them. Peppermint-striped phlox and rubrum lilies nodded in the breeze, with here and there a spike of yellow rue. There was meadow just over the river, and a line of noble trees beyond the meadow, and, high above, some languid puffs of cloud in a clear blue sky. It was too much. We were suddenly unbearably tired.

I said, 'George, my feet are killing me' just as *he* said, 'Honey, I'm sweltering to death.' We smiled at each other. 'Let's go home.'

It was rush hour. Cyclists came swooping down the High like swarms of bees. The big red buses thundered past in series, and motorcyclists ranged along the fringes of each lane, like yapping dogs.

'I will not make a dash for it, dressed this way,' George said.

He didn't have to. A bobby held the pack at bay, and George strode across the street with all the dignity and pride one would expect from a new D.Sc. (Oxon), his red gown belling out in the wind like a cavalier's cape. I patted along behind him, like the Oxford wife I'd seen on that figurine so many months before.

On Magdalen Bridge there was a small party of American tourists sitting on a bench. One of them spotted the oncoming vision in red and jumped to her feet. But George was going too fast for her; he was gone before she'd even got her Box Brownie out of its box. Such a pity, too: in addtion to the gondolier in Venice and the guard on the horse at Whitehall, it would have been so *nice* to have shown the folks at home a snapshot of a Genuine Oxford Don.

It promised to be a fine, hot Fourth of July. Whatever the millions of people at home were setting forth to do today—a trip to the beach, a parade in town, a picnic in the park—one thing was pretty sure: not many of them were going, as we were, to church.

'C'mon, Mom! Pop's got the car out. We've got to be there by nine-fifteen, or all the places will be taken. Cooke warned us, remember?'

We were there at 9.10 a.m., and the places were very nearly taken; the parents of Magdalen College School boys are an eager lot. The Commemoration Service wasn't due to start until ten, but I didn't mind waiting. St Mary the Virgin church was cool and shadowy, and full of history.

Ahead of us a few pews was the pillar whose moulding had been mutilated in 1556, in order to anchor the platform on which Archbishop Cranmer was to stand when he publicly recanted his Protestant opinions. Only he'd reaffirmed his heresy instead. And had gone to the stake. That was during the reign of Bloody Mary, when Roman Catholics had been restored as the state church. But only briefly. The reaction had been Puritanism.

Not that *it* lacked dissenters, either. My eyes strayed to the pulpit across from Cranmer's pillar. In 1606, a young Fellow of St John's had stood in that pulpit and had preached a sermon for which the church authorities had reproved him because it was 'too popish'. But he had persisted in his views. He was William Laud, later Chancellor of Oxford, Archbishop of Canterbury, churchman-turned-statesman. Americans should be grateful to him. It was his Anglicanism that drove the Pilgrims to Cape Cod.

The organ had started to play a Handel overture. It was solemn music; a bit funereal.

Laud, of course, had gone the way of Cranmer. The skullcap he'd worn at his execution is on display at St John's, and his bones lie under the altar of the college chapel. *Except*—I smiled at the thought—*when he and King Charles are bowling*. To dedicate the library he'd added to the college in the seventeenth century, Laud had given a party for Charles I and Queen Henrietta; and now (or so it's said) the ghosts of the two men play bowls there, using their own skulls for balls. One can't see much of the action nowadays, however; they play at the original level of the floor, which has since been raised.

There were the final chords of the introit. The Master was taking his place at the lectern. 'Let us now praise men of renown. . . .' he began, reading from Ecclesiasticus.

Cranmer and Laud. Wesley and Newman. *Like a pendulum swinging across the centuries,* I thought. In the 1730s, John Wesley and his Holy Club had gone from services at St Mary's to his rooms at Lincoln College, where they'd had long, argumentative discussions about Anglican doctrine. John Newman, too, almost a hundred years later, had fallen to wondering what the Established Church really stood for. He'd been Vicar of St Mary's in the 1830s. But the two churchmen, in their separate centuries, had moved in opposite directions—one to found Methodism, the other to lead many of his fellow Anglicans back to Rome. Newman, of course, had died a cardinal.

The choir had sung the 'Jubilate Deo', and now the vicar was beginning the commemoration prayers.

I made the responses abstractedly, reflecting meanwhile that it was an accident of location that had caused so much history to be written in St Mary's. The significant fact was that men who made history had been at the university, and thus at St Mary's. 'Full of grace, and beauty, and scholarship; of reverend antiquity, and ever-young nature and hope': that's what Leigh Hunt had said about Oxford. It was still true, and I was going to miss it.

An English school commemoration is much like an American baccalaureate service. At the conclusion of this one we all streamed up to the Carfax and down St Aldate's to Town Hall, for the second stage of the programme—the Presentation of Prizes. This part was like an American school commencement. The Master made a few remarks, a guest speaker extolled the virtues of scholarship, and the two of them handed out the prizes.

How will I reply, at home, when I'm asked if English schools are better than American ones? First, I thought, *I must make it clear that one can't compare 'the schools', but only the education offered to pupils of comparable abilities . . .*

The Burtons (from New Jersey) were sitting a few seats to our left. They'd invited some of the American families for Sunday supper a few weeks back. The consensus of those with children in grammar schools, that is, the same children who had been on top tracks or in accelerated programmes at home, was that our youngsters had had no real difficulty 'keeping up' with their English classmates, and in some cases were ahead, except in two fields—foreign languages and English.

Instruction in Latin and French seemed to be no better than in the States, but because both languages were begun sooner, English children were ahead of Americans at the same age. That fact struck us as not very important in the long run, since American children stay longer in school. But competence in the use of their own language was something else again; and we were agreed that our children had had far better instruction in English here than they'd had at home. Red had done more written work and it had been more carefully checked than in the States. Essay subjects were more demanding, less 'child-centred', requiring more skilful organization and ability to reason.

The English schoolmasters I had asked were unanimous in saying that American pupils are characteristically unable to order their thoughts as well as English pupils. *We let ours talk too much*, I reflected. The English classrooms I had visited were not so formal as we American parents (conditioned by novels of nineteenth-century schoolboy life) had feared; nevertheless, the master dominates the classroom more than in the United States. There is more consciousness on the part of pupils that an organized body of information is being imparted to them (or dragged out of them) in an organized form.

On the other hand, there certainly wasn't much opportunity for individual research or creative activity in the English schools as in their American counterparts. Janice Poole—the Pooles were from Tennessee—had said, 'I miss finding things out for myself. The mistress just *tells* us, and we write it down.' The pupil artwork I had seen was representational, dull and unimaginative; absent were the uninhibited finger paintings, the zestful collages, the impressionable blob-and-dribble work that even very young children in the States are encouraged to do, not only for self-expression but also to teach appreciation of colour, form and texture.

I was not enthusiastic about the English emphasis on passing exams, either. *Is it worth it to establish a national standard of excellence by this route?* I wondered. *They lose so much.* Even if one ignores altogether the traumatic effect of the 11-plus on children themselves—and one shouldn't, self-esteem being a precious possession for children and adults alike—one can't ignore the harmful pressure exerted by the same exam on the lower schools. The desire to get 'passes' tempts teachers to concentrate on brighter pupils and progressively neglect the less able ones. Nor should one forget the rigidity imposed on a school curriculum by having to prepare pupils for exams over whose content the school itself has no control. If a headmaster must use all the time at his disposal for pounding into his pupils' heads the classical physics needed for a pass at age 16, he's not going to put much emphasis on atomic physics, however desirable he personally believes it might be for citizens of a modern state to understand the difference between fusion and fission.

Yes, but doesn't the United States go too far in the opposite direction? I asked myself. *We have no national standard of the type that exams establish here. Sure, we have the Iowa tests, and the College Boards, and a few others, but no device that prevents enormous variance in the quality of education offered by various school districts. When we are good, we are very, very good. And when we are bad, we are . . .*

I sighed; Red glanced at me sharply and I hastily returned my full attention to the platform. My son had already received two prizes—one for general progress and one for top score in his form's history exam, and now it was being announced that he was first in his division on the General Knowledge paper. George whispered in my ear, 'Not bad for a kid who'd never heard of B.S.T. or "taking silk" nine months ago.' I nodded agreement as Red accepted *The Selected Letters of Sydney Smith* and returned to his seat.

'Another for Marriott,' he murmured at my side. 'He's up with Tinbergen now.'

The two boys, both sixth-formers, were what Americans would call Big Men on Campus. Between them they captained the school teams, sustained the orchestra, various school societies and the Cadet Corps, and served as prefects. *He's the type to be a student-body president, all right,* I thought as Marriott accepted the John Lyne Memorial Prize. *But I still prefer election to appointment.*

There is no student government, in the American sense, in English schools. The Head appoints older students as prefects, who serve as his lieutenants—responsible for school leadership and also for school discipline. I smiled now as I remembered Red's only tangle with a prefect; it had happened in January, when he had mislaid his gym shirt.

The notice on the bulletin board had read: 'The following'—and Red's name led the list—'have lost personal belongings. They will call at the Prefect's Study by Thursday, 12th February.' (Note: no 'please'.)

When Red had gone to get his shirt, the seventeen-year-old prefect—a lad who was a head shorter than Red and still had peach fuzz on his cheeks—had handed over the shirt, and had then said, 'Standard punishment. Fifty lines. Best handwriting. I'll have them tomorrow in break.'

Our independent, almost-grown-up son—I can't think how many years it's been since he's needed 'disciplining'—had swung for a moment between outrage and amusement. He'd settled on the latter, and that night at home he'd meekly written out, fifty times, 'My carelessness with my personal property will cease.'

The next day during recess, as ordered, he had delivered the paper to the prefect, had seen his name checked off a list, and had watched his fifty lines of best handwriting torn in half and dumped in a wastebasket. What's more, his carelessness with his personal property *had* ceased. (At school, anyway.) *But the prefect system,* I thought now, *would never work in the States.*

What was it that our English schoolmaster acquaintance, the one who'd spent the year at the boy's school in New York, had said? Oh yes: 'The boys were alert, friendly, well behaved—and if good manners consist in putting one at ease they had it all over our English children—but nevertheless I found the democracy there a bit wearing. I'm still for a certain amount of benevolent despotism.'

And what was it that Bud Robertson had told me? (The Robertsons were from Iowa.) 'I like my school here fine. Except for one thing. I'll sure be glad to get back to the good discipline at home.' His comment had rocked me back on my heels. It was the *English* schools that were supposed to have such good discipline. The Talbot children, Canadians with an American outlook, had reported that their schoolmates got hit over the knuckles with rulers if they talked out of turn. Red was always having to stay after school because the whole class was being punished for the misbehaviour of one member. I knew that canings, though rare, occurred. So what did Bud Robertson mean by 'good discipline'?

It turned out that he meant *self*-discipline. It made him uneasy to have a class go to pieces whenever the master left the room. He'd been brought up, as most American school children are, with the idea that the teacher and the class are in partnership. From the moment that an American first-grader gets elected Pet Chairman, and with that title acquires the high honour of being allowed to feed the goldfish for a week, his sense of responsibility to the class begins to build. His sense of individual worth builds through those early school years, too. It is a rare American schoolteacher who fails to accord equal, and patient, attention to each child. She wouldn't be human if she didn't have favourites, but I'd never been in an American elementary school classroom without being impressed by the attentiveness the average teacher accords both the fumbling questions of her dull or shy children and the snappy answers of her bright and articulate ones.

The result, by sixth grade, is that if a teacher has to leave the room she leaves a whole class full of ex-chairmen of something or other, each with a vested interest in the *status quo*, and none with a grudge against authority. By the final years in high school the students themselves are calling roll, running the clubs, policing the school, and punishing offenders against the common good. *It's a far less efficient way to run a school than the English system,* I thought now. *But much of the American zest for life, our willingness to take the initiative, our strong sense of responsibility for good works in the community must surely start with that first-grade goldfish bowl.*

I had come to appreciate one of the great strengths in the American school system during this year in England. True, it is only recently that we have begun to give adequate attention to our brightest children—and maybe we will never prize intellectual achievement as highly as practical skills. Perhaps we do give children too much opportunity for self-determination, as

Europeans often allege. *But the wonderful thing about our schools*, I thought now, *is that they are all of a piece with the society that supports them, hence stresses are fewer and easier to resolve than in England.* I had just read Edmund J. King's *Other Schools and Ours*, and remembered his definition of the American school as 'very much a folk institution . . . an extension into the future of the working community itself.' The English schools, on the other hand, reflect the attitudes of just *one* section of 'the working community', the educated upper class, a group that is still so attached to the idea of an intellectual élite, a class trained for leadership, that any other scheme of education seems second-best. *As a result,* I thought, *they have turned the other scheme of education into second-best, and it is going to be a difficult hole for them to get out of.*

I had spent a lot of time informing myself on English school history, especially since 1944, and in visiting schools. I had ticked off some of each type; public, direct-grant, grammar, secondary modern, and London Comprehensive. The inescapable conclusion was that England's educational problems are not likely to be solved as long as schooling and social status remain so inextricably entwined. I had heard no sound educational reason for segregating by sex the grammar school and the public school pupils, or for putting them into uniform, whereas the secondary modern pupils were not. Nor, as long as low-ability children in the public schools manage to learn French and Latin and laboratory science, did there seem to be reason to assume that secondary modern children could not do the same. Yet the assumption underlying the secondary modern schools is that children there are so much less educatable and in other ways so different from other English children that their total school environment should be different.

I remembered that spring, a hot controversy in Oxford over whether the city should build a bilateral school, or a grammar school and a secondary modern school in North Oxford. The people who were against the bilateral proposal had advanced a host of myths in support of their position; that pupils with high academic ability excel pupils with low academic ability in all other areas of accomplishment too; that different teaching techniques are required for secondary modern and for grammar school pupils; that mixing high-ability pupils with average or low-ability pupils must inevitably result in 'holding back the bright ones'. All of those assertions could have been disproved—and right in England, too (the education officer in Leicestershire, where academic segregation is postponed to age 14, and the headmistress of a London grammar school which had been turned into a comprehensive school had both told me that keeping children of all abilities longer together had doubled the number of children capable of doing grammar school work), yet the myths persist, as a useful cover for the main fact: that it is not yet possible for the people in England who really care about education to separate it from the schools' traditional rôle of 'dispensing the norms and graces of the upper classes.' (King's phrase, too.)

The sad thing, I thought now, is that secondary education, as education, is so much better overall than it was before 1944. A pity it had to get mixed up with social class, and the business of having a proper accent. That hopeful phrase, 'parity of esteem', is as hollow as our 'separate but equal'. The main difference is that we discriminate against a minority and the English against a majority.

The last prize had been given now, and we all arose to sing 'Sicut Lilium'. The schoolboy backs I was looking at weren't markedly different from those of a similar gathering at home, except for one thing; none of the skin was brown and none was yellow; none of the eyes was slanted, and none of the noses was broad and flat. None of the names was Wantanabe, or Lopez, or Luzzati, or Sobieski. Not for reasons of prejudice; there just isn't much of anybody in England except the English. They've had no immigration to speak of for hundreds of years. So they don't need to use the schools to unify many and diverse strains of people. *We* still do.

As we eased through the crowd down the Town Hall staircase, George said to Redmond, 'How'd you like to have lunch at the Mitre today? To celebrate your prizes, and the Glorious Fourth? Sure wish we could go to a ball game, too.'

'We *are* going to one,' Red replied, deadpan. 'At least, it's a game that's played with a ball.'

'Cricket's no game. Somebody has to *move* before you can call something a game.'

'Now, Pop. Sometimes there's a lot of action. Anyway, *I* like it.'

I couldn't understand Red's enthusiasm for cricket either.
But I well remember the first real match he'd played in. He'd
come home all fired up, half in glory because he'd been part of
a team and half in agony because he'd made mistakes.

'We were playing against Maltby,' he'd started off. 'And I did
O.K. I really did. Until Rogers started bowling to me. The first
two were wides. The next was a no ball. The fourth looked good,
and I was sure I'd connect real clean and maybe smash it over
the boundary. That would have meant four runs for Wilkinson.
Boy! But what'd I have to go and *do*?' He groaned. 'I went out
hit wicket! And later, when Maltby had their innings and I was
square leg—no, I guess I was silly mid-on—well, *whatever* I was,
here came this ball angling across the pitch. . . .'

'Hold on a minute. Would you mind saying it again, slowly—
and in English?'

'In *English*? Oh. I get you. Sure. It's simple. Cricket's a little
like baseball. There are two sides. First, one side bat, then the
other. Two batsmen are up at a time, one at each end of the pitch.
The pitch is the long, narrow strip of grass with the wicket at
each end, only sometimes the whole field is called the pitch and
the pitch is called the wicket.

'The bowler—that's the pitcher—bowls to one batsman, who
hits the ball if he can. He tries not to knock down his own
wicket, which is what I did—what a goof!—or he's out, which
is what I was. Every time a batsman hits a ball, he and the other
batsman can run, if they want to. They have to change ends to
get a run. Unless one of them hits the ball so it rolls over the
boundary; then his side get four runs. Understand?'

'I'm still with you. Go on.'

'Well, properly, the first side are supposed to keep batting until
all their men are out. Except those who are not out, of course.
Then they go out—the first side, that is—and the other side
come in. Until all their men are out. Except for those *not* out.
Same for both sides, of course. Then they change again, and
again, and maybe twice more. But in our matches there isn't
time to do all this, so each side have only one innings, and there
are only sixteen overs to an innings.'

I was getting a glassy look, but Red didn't notice.

'An over is when the bowler bowls six balls, excluding no balls
and wides. A batsman can be up for quite a few overs. There's

no limit; you're up until you're out. You're out, of course, if somebody catches your hit ball before it strikes the ground. Unless
it's a boundary six. And you're out if you're stumped, bowled,
or leg-before-wicket, too.'

Red paused, looked off into the distance, and then said, 'I think
that's about it, Mom. There are still a few points I'm not clear
on myself. But you get the general idea, don't you?'

'Sure,' I said. 'It's like baseball. Two sides.'

He wasn't listening; he was too full of the game. 'O.K., then.
Now let me tell you what happened next. Maltby was in, and
I was—well, whatever I was—and the batsman hit the ball with
a terrific wallop, and . . .'

As time went on, he learned whether he was square leg or
silly mid-on—and, for that matter, whether he was cover point,
silly mid-off, or short extra cover; they're all fielding positions.
But he never succeeded in making clear to either of his parents
why he was so nuts about the game. All I managed to learn
about it for sure was that nobody ever talks about sticky wickets
while playing cricket. I dutifully watched the game—pardon, a
match—or two, but I still think cricket is like eating a marsh-
mallow sundae or knitting an afghan. Soothing to the people who
are doing it, but not very stimulating to watch.

However, the third phase of Magdalen College School's
'Commem' featured a cricket match between the school team
and the Old Boys—so over we went, at twoish in the afternoon.
The day couldn't have been finer. The playing field lies on an
island in the Cherwell, just below Magdalen Bridge, with the
tower in the distance. The sky was flawlessly blue. Every chair in
the school had been dragged out on the field so that Mums and
Dads could watch the games in ease, and a tea tent had been set
up. We could hear the chirpings of the Parents Association ladies
as they arranged the little cakes on trays and checked the hard-
ness of the ices. And, as a sort of extra blessing, the Magdalen
bells were pealing. Change-ringers go from town to town, having
competitions with the local champions; that's what we must
have heard that afternoon, for the ringing was intermittent. The
sound of bells came and went, muted by distance, as gently
hypnotic as the little wavelets in the river at our feet.

It was a good afternoon, in short, for just sitting and *being*.
We sat and watched the cricket for a bit, and chatted with the

Master, and wandered off to the art exhibit, and strolled back to see if anyone had moved yet on the cricket field—having missed, of course, the afternoon's one flurry of activity. Then a sign went up: 'Teas Now Being Served,' and Red materialized from wherever boys go when they've done their initial duty by their parents at a school event.

'Would you like me to scrum around in there for you?' he said, nodding toward the tea tent.

'Sure,' I said. 'Bring me a pink cake.'

The Schleichers wandered by. They were from Oregon. Twelve-year-old Alan was at M.C.S., and Susan, fourteen, was at a private girls' school. They stopped to chat.

'I hardly recognized you, Susie,' I said. 'You look like an American teen-ager today. Lipstick and high heels. Last time I saw you, you were all done up for St Trinian's.'

Susie giggled. 'I'm out now,' she said. ' "No more classrooms, no more books, no more teachers' dirty looks." ' Then she turned serious. 'Only I don't really mean it. I even think I'm going to miss the uniform—a little. And I sure hated it when I first got here. That *hat*! Ugh!'

Mrs Schleicher spoke. 'Well, I can tell you one thing. It's been wonderful for me to have a year off. No breakfasts gulped while running for the school bus because she's spent so much time deciding what to wear to school. No big scenes because "everyone" is dyeing streaks in their hair, and why can't she? No "May I go here?" "May I go there?" In Oxford, there's no place to go but *home*.'

'Creepers,' said Susan. 'I've probably even forgotten how to dance. C'mon, Al. Let's go get some tea. May we bring you folks something?'

'Red's getting ours, thanks. You'll probably meet him on the way,' I said. 'Just bring something for your mom and dad.'

Bill Schleicher watched his daughter's departing back. 'It's been a particularly good year for her,' he said. 'She wasn't ready to be boy crazy when most of the girls her age were. But you know how it is, at home. You've got to keep up with the crowd. I knew all along she'd be happier wielding a hockey stick along with a lot of other screaming females.'

His wife chimed in. 'You make it sound so simple, Bill. Have you forgotten the stricken look on her face when she first saw that uniform? And those ghastly grey knickers? And how she wept when she didn't get invited to any of the Christmas parties?' Then, to us, 'But Bill's right about it's having been a good year for her, over-all. She really *was* more child than teen-ager, and it was nice for her to get out of that awful competitive, you-have-to-be-popular routine back home. I've decided we put way too much pressure—social pressure, I mean—on our Ameri-can kids.'

We drank our tea in companionable silence, watching the statuesque figures in white on the cricket field, and listening to the Magdalen bells. Then the Schleichers strolled on. George looked at his watch. It was almost four. 'Gosh,' he said, 'I suppose I ought to go to the lab sometime today.'

'I think I'll stick around for a while,' Red announced. 'I'd sort of like to see how the match comes out. It's school forty-seven for three right now. You don't have to stay either, Mom, unless you're especially keen to.'

'I'll run along with Pop, then.'

However, when we got in the car I said, 'How about dropping me off at Longwall, and meeting me in an hour at Balliol? There are a couple of things I'd like to buy, with the packers coming in two days and all. O.K.?'

'O.K.'

I walked up High Street toward the Turl. At the Queen's bus stop, I had to veer to by-pass a lengthy queue. *A bad place to get on*, I thought as I cut past. *Just one queue for all those buses.* It was a transfer point, hence all the buses stopped there. You'd be standing tenth in line when a No. 2 came swooping in, and nobody up ahead would move. So you'd figure they were waiting for 3s or 5s and dart out of line to grab the 2. At which point a retired-colonel type with walrus moustache would take a step forward, then turn and glare because you were being pushy. *Not for me*, I thought. *It's simpler to queue up for the 2 alone, at the Carfax stop.*

George wanted a Balliol tie, and I got it at Walter's. Mr Morrisey knew us by now, and I thought it might be decent to tell him good-bye. He wished us a pleasant journey and thanked us for our custom.

Then I popped into the Market; not that there'd be much left this late in the day at Mrs Palm's.

'I kept back a small loaf of the rye you like,' the jolly little German said.

'That was awfully nice of you, Mrs Palm,' I replied. 'We'll miss you. We're leaving next week.'

'Have a good journey.'

'We'll send you some more Americans.'

'Good. Good.' Big smiles on the other side of the counter. '*Auf Wiedersehen*. God bless.'

The last stop was at the bookstore across from Trinity. They'd had a copy of that Penguin book on *Monumental Brasses*; at least, I was pretty sure that this was where I'd seen it. As I entered, the salesgirl was directing a couple of American tourists to the Shelley Memorial. Guidebook map spread out on the counter, she was saying, '. . . and straight down to the end. Not more than two minutes' walk. Then to your left at All Saints. Look lively after St Mary's, and whenever there's a chance, cross. You'll find Univ where the street widens a bit and begins to curve.'

It won't be nearly as interesting as if they were to cut between Lincoln and Exeter and come down to the High through Radcliffe Square. But I didn't say so aloud. I stood off to one side looking at magazines. And let them go.

How unfriendly of me, I thought, as I took my book and started up the Broad toward Balliol. They were countrymen of mine. They would probably have appreciated hearing an American voice, after the broad a's and dropped h's they'd been coping with. Then I had a flash of insight. *Why, that's the reason I didn't speak! My accent would have equated me with them—and they're TOURISTS. I'm not. I LIVE here.*

My husband was waiting in the car. I scrambled in. 'George,' I said. 'I've just made a discovery. I don't want to go home.'

He turned his head and looked at me, smiled a little, stepped on the starter, then took his hand off the gearshift and patted my knee. 'Don't worry, honey,' he said. 'You'll like it when you get there.'